Brian Robson was born in the United Kingdom in June 1945 and has spent most of his adult life travelling and living in various countries throughout Europe and South East Asia. This book narrates his first travelling experience and his devil-may-care attitude to achieve his wish and return home even if it means risking his life to do so.

I would like to dedicate this book to J. P. Parry and Wayne Robson for their constant support and assistance enabling the story to be told!

Brian Robson

THE CRATE ESCAPE

AUSTIN MACAULEY PUBLISHERS™

LONDON * CAMBRIDGE * NEW YORK * SHARJAH

A CIP catalogue record for this title is available from the British Library.

ISBN 9781528989664 (Paperback)
ISBN 9781528989671 (ePub e-book)

www.austinmacauley.com

First Published (2021)
Austin Macauley Publishers Ltd
25 Canada Square
Canary Wharf
London
E14 5LQ

The Crate Escape is the true story of a teen who, in 1962, emigrated from his hometown, Cardiff, to Australia. His return some eleven months later caused a world-wide stir as he airmailed himself home and became the first and only person ever to fly the Pacific Ocean in a crate. His story is currently being made into a feature film and is the subject of a BBC Television documentary.

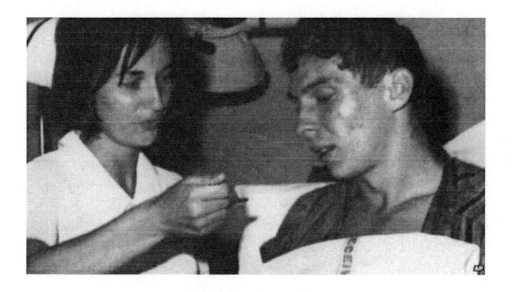

Brian in a hospital in America
© Copyright Channel 4/Reuters

Chapter One
Melbourne, Australia, 1963

Why, oh why, was I here?

It was a question that I had asked myself a hundred times over the months since I had arrived in Australia, and even now whilst walking around the Melbourne exhibition site, I was unable to answer. There were many booths exhibiting British-made products, ranging from furniture to Guinness and from tourism to industry; even shipping lines such as P&O Lines and The Shaw Saville Shipping Company had their services on display. My two friends and I continued to walk around, with me getting more and more depressed with each step I took.

Paul and John, my two mates, looked at me—I must have been showing my feeling of depression—and said, "Come on, Brian, cheer up; the world hasn't ended yet!"

"It may as well have," I grumbled, but to be honest, the sound of their Irish accents seemed to cheer me up a bit.

"I tell you what, let's all have a good old glass of Guinness," said John.

"I don't like Guinness!" I answered with a scoff.

"And neither do I," said Paul, pulling a face.

"Well, just for old times' sake," John insisted. His insistence won the day and going to the Guinness booth, we ordered three glasses of the black stuff.

Paul and John were the same as me, immigrants from the United Kingdom who, for various reasons, had mistakenly chosen to travel to Australia in search of a better life but, after arriving, had found the place not to their liking. We were all about the same age and found solace in commiserating with each other. They were slightly better off than me in that they had been friends since early school days, whereas, I had travelled alone. One big difference between us was that they had virtually made up their minds that they would have to stay the full two years that their contract with the Australian government specified, whereas I was determined to get back to my home in Cardiff, as soon as possible, if not sooner!

The three of us spent most evenings together; they worked for the Victorian Railway and managed to exist in the shack the railway called a hostel. I rented a bedsitter in St Kilda, a suburb of Melbourne, and had just recently started working in a paper mill. The two of them had only been living in Australia a few months, but I had been here for around ten months and originally had also worked for the railway and lived in the same place that they were living in.

We had first met one evening when, after leaving the paper mill which was located near to their place, I had popped into the hostel just to remind myself of how my Australian nightmare had first begun and we three had met in one of the hallways. We had been friends ever since.

We drank the Guinness and continued with our walk around the exhibition hall when we chanced upon a booth that was hosted by a company with the name of Pickford Removals. I stopped dead and the other two bumped into me.

"That company has a depot at the bottom end of my street in Cardiff," I exclaimed. "I always thought that they were just a local business; how wrong can you be!"

"One hundred and one per cent," said John with a grin.

Paul added, "They must be pretty big; their sign says that they move anything anywhere!"

"Pity they can't move us," I chipped in and we all laughed.

Completing our tour of the exhibition, we grabbed a bite to eat before my friends started their short walk back to their hostel and I caught the train back to St Kilda; after all, we had to work the next day, and it was, by now, getting fairly late.

When I arrived back at the bedsitter, I took a shower, and then I lay down on the bed. Unable to sleep, I tossed and turned, with my mind constantly returning to the Pickford Removals' booth I had seen a few hours earlier. Would it be possible? I kept asking myself. I mean even to me it seemed a bit far-fetched.

Far-fetched or not, it was worth a try. I got off the bed and scribbled down a few notes before attempting to go to sleep again. As soon as dawn broke, I was up, dressed and out of the bedsitter. I quickly walked to the station to catch the train into Central Melbourne and to pay a visit to a certain airline's office. So eager was I that I arrived before the office had opened, and so, whilst hanging around outside, I constantly checked my scribbled notes so that I would memorise the questions that I wanted to ask without forgetting my lines. Finally, the doors were opened, and I went inside the building with the feeling of urgency, desperately hoping to get positive answers to my questions.

Inside, a few desks greeted visitors, with each having a single chair behind it for a Qantas agent to sit on. Two chairs were placed at the front of each desk from where people could make inquiries or book tickets, each having a sign above reading 'Passenger Inquiries'. These were not for me, and it was a few moments before I spotted a stand-up counter with a sign that read 'Freight Inquiries'. Knowing my rightful place in life, I walked up to the counter and spoke to the man standing behind it.

"Hi, can you help me?" I asked cheerfully.

"I can try," he answered. "What help do you need?"

"My company has sent me here to ask about sending freight to London; I've made a few notes," I said before I pulled my scribbles out of my pocket. "Okay, if I ask you a few things?"

"That's why I'm here; fire away," he said, and I started to read from the notes I had made the previous evening.

I did not go to work that afternoon but thoughtfully sat in a milk bar, considering the answers I had received from the agent and waiting for my two Irish friends to finish their daily grind. I was extremely excited about my morning's visit, and I just couldn't wait to meet up with them again.

Keeping a careful eye on the time, I waited until I knew that they would have returned to the hostel before leaving the milk bar and walking there to meet them. With a quick tap on the door and without being invited, I walked into the room and sat on Paul's bed. He glanced up from the magazine he was reading, smiled and in his broad Irish accent said, "You're early this evening?"

I told them that I hadn't been to work and that instead, I had paid a visit to the airline office of Qantas. "Thinking of doing some travelling?" John asked jokingly.

"With your help, I might be," I answered with a smile.

I had their full attention immediately; I could almost see the inquiring look in their eyes. Knowing that I had extraordinarily little money, Paul asked, "Are you serious?"

"I've never been more serious; listen, fellas! I think I know a way to get back to the UK without having to pay the fare to travel over there, or money to travel from there and—more importantly, do it without a passport!"

10

Now they both were all ears, and I had their attention.

"Do you remember the Pickford sign at the exhibition yesterday, the one that read 'We move anything, anywhere'?" They both nodded their heads.

"Don't tell me you're going to ask Pickford to move you back to the UK." Laughed John.

"Not quite." I smiled. "With your help, I'm going to do it myself!"

"What the hell are you talking about?" asked John, by now completely confused.

"I'm going to airmail myself to London," I said, trying to sound confident.

"And you want us to stick the stamps on?" John giggled.

"Not quite; I want Paul to help me with a wooden crate and you to help me with some paperwork."

"Sure, if we hurry and get a crate now, we might catch the last post!"

"If you don't shut up and listen to me, they may play the last post—for you!" I growled back.

John stopped joking and they both listened to what I had to say about my visit to Qantas Airlines earlier that day. After I finished talking, I asked if they would both help me to put my plans into action. Paul agreed that he would help whilst John gave a resounding "no"!

"Why not, why can't you help?" we both asked him at the same time.

"Because it won't work, for one thing, how are you going to breathe? Don't think that aircraft holds are the same as in passenger cabins at thirty-thousand feet."

"I'll manage that part; you just need to help when I'm on the ground." Making a huffing sound with his mouth and ignoring my answer, he continued,

"Anyway, it would be too costly to send a crate all that way; where's the money supposed to be coming from?"

"Cash on delivery; to be paid in London?"

"I'd help with most things, but don't ask me to kill you!"

"I won't die. I'll make sure that it works. Anyway, I'd only be in there for about forty-eight hours."

"That's about forty-seven hours and fifty-five minutes longer than you'll need to die!"

Later that evening, Paul told me not to worry. He was sure he could persuade John to help us!

Chapter Two

After making up my mind to go ahead with my plan, the first thing to do was to find a suitable wooden crate in which to travel; this proved to be harder than it had at first appeared to be. I went all around Melbourne searching but kept coming up with nothing.

The biggest problem was the size; it needed to be large enough for both me and my suitcase to fit comfortably in and yet, Qantas regulations said that it couldn't be any larger than 36"x24"x18". There was also a maximum weight restriction; however, I was quite skinny; the suitcase didn't weigh much, and even allowing for the crate itself, we would easily fit in that allowance.

Although the crate needed to be lightweight, it still needed to be strong after all, the plan wouldn't work if two men picked it up from the top and I fell out of the bottom!

After a few days of searching and coming up with nothing, Paul suggested that we could make one ourselves. I vetoed that idea on the grounds that none of us was a carpenter and also, we would need to buy extra tools and that, considering the small amount of money I had, would prove too expensive.

I had tried everywhere I could think of with absolutely no success when one day, whilst on a Melbourne tram, I passed by something that looked like a small timber yard that I had not yet explored. I jumped off the tram at the next stop and quickly walked back to where I had seen planks of wood piled up outside a pair of wooden gates. Inside, there were stacks of wood in all sizes, and although the material was there to make a crate, I couldn't see one already made. Paul's idea of starting from scratch was beginning to re-surface in my mind when I almost bumped into the guy who was working in the place.

"Hi, do you sell wooden crates?" I asked him.

"Not really," he said, then as an afterthought, he asked, "What do you want it for?"

"I want to ship some small gifts to the UK."

"We might have one, if it's still here," he said as an afterthought, whilst walking me to the back of the building. As we passed around a stack of wood there, sitting in a small corner was the most beautiful wooden crate I had ever seen!

Controlling my excitement (a show of delight may have increased the price) I asked him how much he wanted for it? He started off at five pounds and I gradually got him down to three pounds ten shillings before asking him if he had a tape measure.

It measured in at just under the maximum size I needed and so, without any more ado, I bought and paid cash for it.

The next step was to get it back to my bedsitter, and for this, the guy phoned a taxi truck for me—taxi trucks in Melbourne were vehicles that you phoned as you would a taxi but were meant for instantly moving small freight or packages from anywhere to anywhere within the city.

At the rear of the house in which my bedsitter was located was a plot of land owned by the landlady who rented out the bedsitters. It was separated from the garden of the house by a wooden fence which had a few panels missing and if you weren't too fat, you could easily squeeze through the gap and onto the land. The place was surrounded by other buildings except for one side leading onto a street, and this was secured by a large gate preventing people without permission from entering. It was the perfect place to keep and work on our project, and so, a few days before I bought the crate, I had told the landlady that I and my friends were sending gifts back to the UK and could I store a box out there? She was rather fat and grumpy and never agreed with much, but I had used my charms to persuade her to allow us to do so.

The taxi truck, with me sitting next to the driver, delivered the crate, and after I had opened the gate, I had helped the driver to offload it before making sure that I got his telephone number for future use. Later in the day, I went over to the hostel to meet John and Paul and ecstatically informed them that part one of my journey to nowhere had been completed! After further discussions, we then arranged that Paul would come over to my bedsitter the following Saturday to help me with the second part.

Saturday arrived and the two of us worked together performing multiple tasks. Using a string, we plaited it together until it formed a thin rope, then, after cutting it into small sections, we nailed the ends into the crate to form our version of a safety belt to prevent my body being thrown around if the crate was handled roughly. We bought two bottles, filled one with water and left the other one empty—in case I needed to pass water! These were fastened in the crate along with an old torch that we found. A book of Beatles songs was thrown in as reading material and the final item that would be secured inside was an old hammer that I would use to help me escape the box after I had arrived in London.

We met up with John later in the evening to inform him precisely what help was needed from his department. John was working in a ticket office and had access to both a typewriter and some Victorian Railway letterheads. Using both, we needed him to prepare the paperwork that was needed to accompany the crate. I needed two copies of a waybill stating what was inside the box plus an invoice type document that, most important of all, stated that the box would be collected at London's Heathrow Airport, and that on collection the collector would pay the full cost of the freight charges. John, under protest, agreed to do this the next Monday – that being the next workday after our meeting. One question needed answering before the paperwork could be completed, and that was to decide what we would claim to be inside the crate. John, thinking he was the clever one, suggested: "One idiot, dead on arrival." However, we settled for 'mainframe computer parts for repair' in the belief that nobody knew much about computers (ourselves included), and so some noisy official was less likely to poke his nose around inside the box.

After we had made notes to remind John what he had to type we all went to a local stationery shop where I managed to purchase some pre-printed signs that read 'This side up' and 'Fragile: Handle with Care' so I could nail them to the crate later. The rest of the weekend was spent relaxing, well relaxing as much as possible, knowing that I was about to have a very un-relaxing time the following week.

Monday arrived, and I could not wait for Paul and John to join me at my bedsitter after they had finished their work for the day. We were all really delighted with John's handiwork; all the documents looked professional; at least, they did to us, bearing in mind that we had never seen this type of documents before.

I decided that I was going to leave on Wednesday and spent the next day and a half with knots in my stomach. The knots were caused through nerves. I can honestly say I was scared stiff, and by having taken some laxatives in the belief that if I cleaned out my system, I wouldn't need to go to the toilet in the crate!

My two friends stayed away from work for two days pretending to be sick and both stayed with me for most of that time. It felt like a wake with none of us really knowing quite what to say to each other. They were as nervous as I was!

On Tuesday, I had phoned Qantas and informed them about a crate that would be delivered to Melbourne Airport and they had assured me that if it was delivered to the Qantas Freight Shed before 12 o'clock midday on Wednesday, it would catch that day's flight to London. I also contacted 'Taxi Trucks' and arranged for them to come to the gate entrance of the land behind my bedsitter to take the crate (and me) to the airport and to be there at quarter past ten in the morning.

Wednesday arrived! I packed my suitcase and tied it into the crate, then took the pillow off my bed and put it in to support my back. Only then I got in it and sat down just to make doubly sure that there was still room for me. As I sat down, I heard the familiar voice of my landlady shouting at John and Paul: "What are you two doing here?" I quickly stood up and saw her head poking through the hole in the fence—she was far too fat to get through it.

I shouted back to her, "We're getting this crate ready to go to London, remember me telling you?" She made a huffing and puffing noise before pulling her head back into the garden of the house.

Just to make sure that she had gone, I got out of the box, walked to the hole and poked my head around the fence; she was nowhere to be seen; the coast was clear!

It was getting late, and so I gave my friends a final hug and sat down in the crate. They nailed the lid on tight whilst telling me I could still change my mind and continually asking if I was all right. Suddenly, they went quiet, and I knew the taxi truck had arrived. The driver asked them if it was very heavy, then tried to move it with his hands. He gave up and got a small forklift from the truck. It was a weird feeling as the crate began to move; John whispered, "Good luck!" and I was on my way!

Chapter Three

The taxi truck rumbled along the road leading to Melbourne Airport where we arrived about an hour later. Using a larger forklift, Qantas staff took the crate off and placed it on the tarmac. Although dark inside the box, I could see out through the small gaps between the planking that formed the crate. Stupidly, I began to wonder if the people milling around could see into it and see me inside, they obviously could not as they just proceeded to complete their work. I was left alone for about an hour before I heard a shout, "This one is for Sydney," and I started to move again.

I sensed, rather than saw, that I was being placed inside an aircraft, and then everything went black. I could still hear people's voices but couldn't see anything, no light, just complete darkness. Gradually, the voices stopped, and silence prevailed. Another ten minutes passed before the deafening roar and slight vibration of the plane's engines filling the air. I could feel movement, and we were bumping over the taxiways before the engine sounds grew to a high-pitched scream as we raced down the runway. A few more minutes and we were airborne. I felt scared and at the same time elated; my journey to London had begun.

Just over an hour later, we landed in Sydney and the crate was loaded onto an airport truck. We travelled a short distance before being picked up and dumped upside down on the ground. Suddenly, from being in a seated position I was "standing" on my head and neck! The idiots! The crate was marked 'this side up' and yet they had taken no notice of the signs I had placed on it at all. I was half inclined to get out of the crate, turn it up the right way then, before getting back in, telling Qantas staff exactly what I thought of them! I giggled at this idea before someone walking past forced me to shut up and keep quiet!

My neck began to get extremely painful, and a headache set in. I tried to turn myself around and into a sitting position but, with the lack of space and my safety rope holding me, it proved impossible. I was stuck in that position until someone turned the crate over and followed the direction of the stickers that I had put on it by turning it back into a position where I could be seated again.

As the minutes turned into hours, I kept telling myself that it wouldn't be too much longer until they moved me into the aircraft that would take me to the UK when hopefully, whoever did the moving would be able to read and put the crate facing up in the direction that it was marked.

As the hours ticked by things were getting worse with my head feeling as if it would burst and my neck, taking all my body weight, feeling that it was about to snap. I began wondering that if they treated me like this, just how badly they were treating the other passengers?

Then it dawned on me that I was not even a passenger yet and looking at my watch I realised that they would not even be departing on time. By now, they should have been serving drinks and a meal, and yet I was still on the ground!

Night-time had descended and with it came a cold wind, which the slight gaps between the slats of the crate allowed to enter. Not only was my head and neck at breaking point but I was beginning to shiver with the cold. I swore that I'd never fly this airline again and that any future crate trips would only be booked with one of their competitors—that would teach them!

The night wore on, and it was only by my cracking jokes to myself that I kept going. However, it came to the stage when even the jokes didn't make me laugh anymore or take the pain away. Another worrying point was that by now I should have been well on the way to the UK and yet, I was still sitting uncomfortably here in Sydney.

Twenty-four excruciating hours had passed before someone put me out of my misery. As suddenly as it had been turned upside down, the crate was turned the right way up again, loaded onto a forklift and taken on a joyride around the airport. During my tour, I could not resist trying to massage my neck as much as possible by moving my arm across my chest in an upward direction and using my hand to squeeze the left side and the back. It didn't make much difference really, but it was better than nothing. Luckily, I was able to keep squeezing both my shoulders by using one arm at a time and holding each in the same position across my chest whilst using my hands to squeeze the muscles; it seemed to help ease the pain.

My mode of transport and I were lifted into what I could only imagine was the hold of a plane. The crate was placed (thankfully, the right way up) on the floor of the aircraft and then with more noises, other freight was loaded. As more and more crates were put on board, the light disappeared into the darkness and the sounds became muffled to the extent that they finally stopped altogether, and everything went deathly silent.

After about half an hour the aircraft started moving and then came to a stop. The roar of the engines sounded deafening and was followed by further movement of the 'plane accompanied by the rumble of wheels on the concrete. One more stop and the surge of the plane rushing forward followed by the feeling of lifting into the sky gave me cause to congratulate myself; my plan was working. Despite the pain, I was leaving Australia!

As the drone of the engines went on and on, breathing became harder, and I soon learnt to suck the air in using short sharp gulps. However, a much more worrying problem was beginning to show itself; I was developing big pains in my neck, back and especially in my knees. Sitting in an upright position I was unable to stretch my legs; they were permanently folded into my chest and my knees were getting bad cramps. I could, however, with a struggle, bend my legs even further into my chest and then place the flat of my feet against the bottom side of the crate. Pressing each foot against the wood caused even more knee pains, but it seemed to ease up considerably when I lowered my feet and stopped torturing myself. After a further five minutes, I would repeat the action until it eventually became impossible to move my legs.

Some hours later, I could feel the plane descending—although I had no idea where we were—I felt myself being landed and taxied. After we had stopped moving, I heard the doors to the hold opening, followed by voices in a language that I didn't recognise. Obvious noises of freight being moved in and out followed before and with the plane still on the ground, I dozed off to sleep.

I was awakened by a frightening noise, the sound of dogs growling and barking! They would make a scuffling sound then growl before repeating the exercise. I was sure they knew that I was there. I could hear the handler talking to them and I could only thank God that those dogs could not speak, otherwise, my escape plan would have ended there and then!

It didn't take long before we were airborne again, and I imagined that a steward or stewardess was going to have a hard time bringing me a drink and a meal; it would not be easy attending to passengers who were travelling in their own crate! Joking to myself did not seem to be working anymore either. I barely remembered the following landings or take-offs. My whole body was racked with indescribable pain and my head was about to burst open. I didn't know if I was too hot or too cold as it seemed to me that my temperature was changing by the minute. I was beginning to fall in and out of reality, forgetting where I was and what I was supposed to be doing. Just becoming more and more confused and uncaring by the hour.

The plane was in trouble and could crash land; the only way to keep it airborne was to lighten the load. The captain asked for volunteers, anyone who would jump out and make the aircraft lighter. No one offered. The captain then told the crew to throw the entire luggage out of the plane. Struggling, they managed to get every bag out, but we were still going down. Only one thing left—the freight!

"Throw it all out," ordered the captain. Following his orders, they came to my crate; they manhandled it to the door of the hold. I could see the sea thousands of feet below, and I shouted to warn them that I was in the box; they took no notice, so, I started to scream at them. I had to stop the crate being thrown out. If the fall did not kill me, I would drown; drowning in the large expanse of water below scared the life out of me. I screamed and screamed but still everyone ignored me either not knowing or not caring that I was in there, stuck in a box! Did I just dream it or was it happening? I had no idea and no way of finding out the truth from the fiction!

How did I get in this mess in the first place…?

Chapter Four

Cardiff, United Kingdom, 1962

Cardiff, in 1962, was a dismal place. Entertainment was virtually non-existent and even the pubs were closed on Sundays to allow the locals to attend church without being too inebriated! Entertainment consisted of watching television shows in glorious black and white with broadcasting closing around 10:30 at night as allowing mere natives to watch after that time might result in their oversleeping the following morning and causing their employers to lose money by their not attending work!

On Saturday night, teens could if they had enough money, treat themselves to the local cinema. We actually had three in the town centre, and the Top Rank had opened a dance hall which could be attended by all those over the age of eighteen who had, or could, scrounge enough money to pay the admission fees.

Most of the money that local teens managed to spend at the Top Rank was obtained from a wage which could at best be described as downright dismal, borrowed from mates or, if one was lucky, borrowed from some unsuspecting richer teen who didn't need it as much as the mate who borrowed it. That was the alternative of taking them with you and resorting to a type of begging activity to try and get them to pay whilst still pleading that you didn't have enough money to get into the place.

It seemed that most days were either spoilt by incessant rain, making you spend what little money you had on a raincoat to keep the nasty stuff away or on bright, glorious days with lots of sunshine when of course, you would be busy working to help pay for the raincoat that you so desperately needed the day before. All in all, it was a pretty drab sort of existence supported by the publicised fact that had you been born a few years earlier, you may have lost what little life you had, fighting for a king and queen who you'd never met and for a country that you were not particularly in love with either!

On the 4th of June 1963, I reached the right old age of eighteen and realised that my whole life was before me. The cinema every Saturday, the Top Rank once a month and a new raincoat every year! What else did one need to benefit from the joys of life? After carefully thinking over that question, I arrived at the conclusion that the answer was much more, the only problem being how to get it?

On my eighteenth birthday, I started work in a new job. I had applied for the position when I was seventeen and the company had agreed to employ me but not until I had turned eighteen due to the fact that I would need a licence to perform my duties, and this licence was only available to people after they had reached that ripe old age. I got the licence, and my salary increased from around four pounds per week to a hefty ten pounds with the opportunity to travel daily all around the Vale of Glamorgan.

I had finally achieved my ambition and aspired to the illustrious position of no less than bus conductor with the Western Welsh Omnibus Company!

My life had made a complete turnaround, and now, I was touring all around the country regularly visiting the towns of Penarth, Barry Island and sometimes even Bridgend in addition to most of the Rhondda Valley! I was taking people on holiday and to work, people who mostly were earning a lot less than me! If I had thought Cardiff was dull, I now had a different view on life. The Rhondda Valley made Cardiff look like a real city even on one of its rainiest of days; now I had something to compare the place with. Hills and mountains, so what, we had cinemas! Coal tips? Nothing, mate, we had a Top Rank Ballroom, and we had pubs, many of them! I never mentioned that they were closed on Sundays, well in all fairness, so were theirs!

So, many things had improved. I say many things because one bugbear was still around. You see, I lived with my parents, and that was a big problem.

I was born in June 1945, and just one month before that, Adolph Hitler had managed to lose the Second World War. Not really a problem for a one-month-old baby, you may truthfully think? You'd be right; my problem was not exactly the war. It was that the end of the war freed up my father and allowed him to return to MY home! I say my home because at that time of my life, it seemed to me that I owned everything that I could get my hands on. On arriving home from fighting the 'Hun' and looking at his new-born son, it was true to say it was hate on both sides, a problem that neither of us ever managed to solve throughout our entire time of living together. He thought he was still fighting the Germans and as there was no one small enough for him to pick on, I became the enemy.

The fact that the 'Huns' had blown the roof off our house was entirely my fault; he believed that rationing of food had been implemented by me, and on his return from his all-empowering conquests of war, there was another male in what was his domain! He might have taken some responsibility for that but, in his eyes, it was still my fault! He paced around thinking he was the male lion controlling his pride and that pride had no room for another male regardless of its age. When the lioness was not looking or had been distracted, one could expect him to take a quick swipe. Much better to kill it or take away any chance it had of succeeding and possibly taking over his domain; little did he know that the more he tried to curtail my actions, the more devious I became in order to survive!

Many, many times when I was young, he used to find a reason to cause trouble. In fact, most times he did not even need a reason. Me not asking permission to leave the table at mealtimes, eating too fast, eating too slow even, not wanting to eat at all were reasons in his mind to take his belt off and use it on me. We used to do a kind of dance where he would hold onto my wrist whilst knocking me around with his belt. It was a funny kind of dance routine: BASH, then my legs would take me around in a circle with him holding on to me, BASH, then another dance around in a circle; a number of times I wished that when he took his belt off, his trousers would fall down! No such luck! He managed to keep them up. The strange thing was that my mother just sat there watching; maybe she was wishing that for a different reason his trousers would fall too!

Things never got any better at home; in fact, the more money I earned the worse it became. Not the belt, of course I had grown much too big for that, so it was superseded by many arguments some of which I might have been slightly responsible for by over advertising that I was now earning as much money as he was, but I could spend mine as I wanted, and he had a house and family to keep. That is not to say I didn't pay my share; two pounds ten shillings every week went to my mother and absolutely nothing to him! I didn't hesitate to make sure that he knew I was wasting my money on whatever I wanted and whenever I wanted to. I think that this early spending might be partly to blame because, even to this day, I like to spend money, lots of it.

Time passed, and I put up with the problems at home by still living there but staying away as much as possible and after all, I got on well at work and by working shifts I didn't have to see that much of him. Whenever we did meet, he always managed to dream up as many insults as his simple brain would allow him to; insults that were always twisted around by me and thrown back at him in the hope of scoring a direct hit!

At work, sunny, or rainy days didn't seem to matter anymore as I was safely ensconced in the back of the bus with plenty of people to chat to. Older or younger passengers were all to be found there. I just had to collect the fares, then sit down and chat with them. In those days, even the drunks on the late shifts were friendly. If there were no passengers, I still had the beautiful industrial estates, slag heaps or cloudy streets and roads to look at and at the same time dream that next Saturday was Top Rank night.

That was, of course, unless I was working a late shift on Saturday or Sunday, but even then, there was always the weekend after, and I was getting paid every Friday which meant that I always had money!

The Western Welsh Omnibus Company was not a bad place to work after you had slowly adjusted to the shift work that was. With buses leaving the depot all day and night, you really never quite knew where you would be; have you ever been late for work and travelling on the bus when the thought hits you— how come you can be late, but bus drivers and conductors were always on time? They are not! To allow for the fact that in those days, bus crews often had to walk to and from work, mostly in the early morning or late at night; many were late. To compensate for this, companies would operate 'standby crew'. If you managed to fall out of bed at almost the same time that sane people were just about retiring for the night, then walked about four or five miles in rain, snow or whipping winds, you could arrive at the depot and play one-arm bandits whilst drinking gallons of tea and waiting for the duty inspector to inform you that someone had failed to 'fall' out of bed and you had the pleasure of taking a bus on route 303 or whatever. For the remainder of the day, you would be travelling back and forth between the Rhondda Town of Mardy and Cardiff General Bus Station whilst for most of the time, dreaming of the one-arm bandits still waiting for you to play with them at the bus depot!

Summer on the buses was spectacular; most of Wales—or so it seemed— were on holiday and determined to get the most out of the weather by travelling with large families to the coast and seaside resort of Barry Island. Sand, sea, and a large fairground, all wafted over by the sticky smell of candyfloss. A great day was assured, at least for the holidaymakers who didn't worry too much about having to stand for the entire journey between Cardiff and the coast as all the buses, including the many extras laid on, were completely full and overcrowded.

For the bus conductors who could manage to put up with yelling kids, things were not too bad. Get on the bus, signal the driver that you are full and under threat of death, not to stop at any other stops. Issue seventy-three-day return tickets each to the value of two shillings and three pence (one and two pence for kids), then retire to the bus platform and dream of how much money you could win on those one-arm bandits still back at the depot!

One-arm bandits was a very choice name for those machines because they would rob you blind! They did help you pass the time whilst waiting for your next bus, but hardly ever did they allow you to win. However, they did give the bus company the chance to collect back some of the money that they had paid you in wages. That was until one day…

My driver Jack, a full load of passengers and I, had travelled along the exhilarating route from Cardiff to the Rhondda Town of Mardy. Passing the coal mines and slag heaps, that were the highlights of the journey, we eventually arrived at the terminus located outside the Mardy Working Men's Club where, as usual, we had twenty minutes to wait before going back down the mountain through Pontypridd and onwards to the megacity of Cardiff.

The club, in one of their rare business endeavours, had managed to make and sell tea, at three pence a cup, to the bus drivers and conductors who had managed to survive the arduous journey up their sacred mountain!

In addition to the business of selling tea, some bright spark had installed a few one-arm bandits in the club's lobby which, although they were meant for club members the visiting bus crews were encouraged to use, more as a way of extracting money from the visitors than expecting them to win.

Jack and I, each purchased a cup of tea and settled down to spend some money by playing the bandits. At six pence a go, we had spent maybe two shillings and sixpence between us when, much to our surprise, the machine started making all sorts of weird noises and throwing money out and all over the place. This by itself was unbelievable as no one in living memory had ever seen a machine actually pay out more than a few shillings at most but the jackpot, the whole jackpot. This was indeed a miracle!

A miracle that was not lost on the natives and club members who entered the club lobby in droves, growling under their breath that the mighty Western Welsh Omnibus Company was stealing their money. Not a thought was given to the fact that bus crews used those machines every time they bought the club's teas and that in reality more money had been gambled by visiting drivers and conductors than the whole of the Welsh coal-mining fraternity combined!

Jack and I quickly gathered all the money that the machine had thrown at us and dumping it in my conductor's money bag, we slowly made a nonchalant retreat whilst pretending not to hear the rising sound of growls coming from an assembled crowd that collectively could have filled a Welsh rugby ground!

We ran the last few feet to the bus, still clutching the money bag, jumped on and sped away. I continually kept looking to see if we were being followed by a horde of ex-rugby players! We didn't stop at any bus stop until we reached the comparative safety of Pontypridd where the duty inspector approached and asked us what we thought we were doing?

"Going to Cardiff?" I suggested with an innocent grin.

"Well, you're not supposed to have left Mardy yet." He snapped back. "Is your watch broken?"

"No, but it looked like it was going to rain, and we didn't want to get wet." I offered as a feeble excuse.

"Rain, rain?" He went red in the face as if he were about to explode. "Rain, since when did it matter if the bloody bus gets wet? Now I've heard everything except which idiot told you to make sure the bus stays dry!" Unable to think of anything else to say, he then added, before mumbling to himself and walking away, "Wait here until you're timed to leave!"

Jack asked me what he had to say, and I told him that we had to stay in Pontypridd until the bus got dry. I got another funny look from Jack, but while we were waiting, I counted our winnings, and we shared an amazing six pound ten shillings between us. We never again bought a cup of tea in Mardy Working Men's Club and never played their one-arm bandits either; in fact, the thought of those Welsh miners growling at us was permanently etched in my mind!

The summer was slowly ending and as holidaymakers began to finish their holidays and return to work, the overtime that bus crews were earning slowly came to an end. That's not to say I was complaining; I was still earning a reasonable salary and had gradually got used to the walk to and from home at the start and end of each day's shift.

My sister and her husband used to live with us but after having a baby, they moved out leaving just me, my mother, and my father together in the house. I say together, but that was never the case or even the correct word to use. As a family, we were never together and were completely dysfunctional. My mum, who was also pregnant, was reasonably okay, but father was still fighting his own private war and using every available moment to cause problems.

The pair of them were members of the local labour club which was a working men's club selling cheap beer but with a much posher name. Every Saturday and Sunday night, the club would throw in bingo and some form of entertainment and my father, who had proudly been elected as the entertainment secretary or some such thing, had a duty to attend. The beer might also have had something to do with that decision. Mother also wanted to go as well but by now she had had the baby, and so a babysitter was required.

I was the first choice, and whenever I was available, I was press-ganged into looking after my baby brother. To be honest, I wasn't too perturbed by this except for the many rows and arguments that took place between my father and me throughout the week. The one chance I had to get retribution for all the problems he was causing me was to positively refuse to babysit. When the idea that I wasn't going to do it anymore finally sunk in, they managed to press-gang my father's older sister, who was a spinster, to take over the job. She appeared quite happy to accept the challenge as if nothing else it got her out of her house over the weekend and she received free meals. However, it never stopped the arguments between him and me, and if anything, they only got worse!

Apart from the constant arguments where he was always right and everyone else was wrong (he argued with my mother almost as much as he argued with me), there was a problem of things going missing and, needless to say, I always got the blame. The fact that he gambled on horses often and liked to drink, with both pursuits costing money, was never taken into consideration by anyone at the time; if it had been, maybe I wouldn't have taken the blame for his wrongdoings as at that time I didn't gamble, hardly ever drank and anyway had more money than he did.

I think that toward the end of that period and certainly in later years, my mother had seen the light and deep down knew who the guilty person was! I suppose in truth, although I gave my mother money every week, I would never give or lend him a penny, it didn't help matters one iota but just gave him more reason to seek revenge on me. I still believe to this day, many years later, that he was the most horrible person I ever knew, and I expect that if he were still alive, he would say the same thing about me.

I had, on one or two occasions, thought of looking at somewhere else to live, but in those days, most landlords didn't like the idea of an eighteen-year-old boy renting their property, and that was quite apart from the fact that most places available to rent were not exactly nice places to live in; well, certainly not for teens who were perhaps used to more space in which to do their own thing regardless of how much trouble it caused.

Apart from all that being considered, who would wake me up for work in the morning?

One morning, someone had woken me up, my mother I guess; well, it would have to have been as the only time he came in my bedroom was to search for money or anything he could sell. I had left for work and was sitting in the bus garage reading a copy of the local paper. The news was not that interesting, and I was just about to throw away the offending publication when something caught my eye.

Chapter Five

Glancing through the classifieds in the newspaper there were various adverts for the usual types of consumer products one would normally see advertised followed, in the employment section, by a few jobs available. The local steel mill was looking for staff as were several other employers who were offering equally boring jobs. My attention was suddenly attracted to one advert where the advertiser was seeking employees to work on the railway. I laughed to myself as I thought of the poor travelling public. I mean our bus service was bad enough, but compared to the railway, we were nothing but bloody angels!

Mumbling to myself, I wondered why I was looking at it, after all, working on any form of public transport was pretty much the same, and I already had a job on the buses. However, I continued to read until I finally realised that the advertised positions were in Victoria.

Who wants to live in London, I thought? Victoria Station might be a good place to work, but London was expensive; besides, I had nowhere up there to live. I still carried on reading, and it was only near the very bottom of the advert that I suddenly realised that the job on the railway was not in London but in Victoria—Australia!

Australia, I smiled at the thought. The money they were offering was better than I was currently earning here, and it would get me away from the slag heaps of the Rhondda Valley, and surprise, surprise it would also get me away from the house or at least the person that, in my mind, was ruining my life.

They were holding interviews for the next two days in a building opposite Queen Street Railway Station which was Cardiff's second railway station and, in a building, known as the Masonic Hall. These were walk-in interviews; no appointment necessary, just turn up!

I had a two or three-hour break that afternoon and so, after ripping the advert out of the newspaper, I jumped on a bus that was leaving the depot and heading in the general direction of the bus station. From there, it was an easy walk to the building where the interviews were being held. As I was walking it started raining so, pulling up the collar of my Western Welsh uniform, I made my way to the interview. I did not really mind getting wet, but I hated having a damp shirt collar.

The advert had said nineteen years of age and older, but I didn't think that it would matter very much, as I'd be old enough in June and that was just three months away. In any case, they could say no for many reasons, and just going for an interview didn't automatically mean that even if I was offered, I'd take the job.

Soaking wet I arrived outside the building and pulled my coat collar down to make myself look respectable before I gingerly entered the building.

"Excuse me," I said to the first official-looking figure to come into view, "is this where they are holding interviews for Australia?" With a brief nod of the head, he pointed me across the room to a table and an empty chair. Gingerly, I approached the chair before being scanned up and down by an older smiling man who then asked me to take a seat.

"Thinking of changing your life, are you, young man?" He smiled.

"Well, yes," I mumbled, remembering at the last minute to smile back.

"Are you employed now?"

"Yes," I answered looking down at my uniform.

"Where do you work?"

"Western Welsh, I'm a bus conductor." I gushed back at him.

At this point, I was half expecting him to wish me a good day and inform me that he had no vacancies for bus conductors but, to my sheer surprise, he started to inform me of the abundant job opportunities that he had to offer. With my experience in public transport, I was exactly what they were looking for! I thought he was going to offer me the Managing Directors position!

I was tempted to ask if they had slag heaps in Australia the same as we had in the Rhondda Valley but thought better of it and kept my mouth tightly shut.

He carried on in his Australian accent, and before everything he said had fully sunk in, there I was, signing various documents and being whisked behind a screen where I was poked and prodded by two doctors before being pronounced healthy, fully fit, and still living. Returning to my smiling gentleman, I again sat down, and he formally offered me the job. There and then! I'd got a new job in Australia!

For a few moments, I really thought that they were going to immediately send me but was greatly relieved to hear that I had to wait at least a further three months until I was nineteen. After all, I reasoned to myself the problem with leaving the same day was that I had an afternoon shift to finish and did not even have a suitcase with me! Well, one didn't usually carry one's possessions with one when working an afternoon shift even if you did live in Cardiff.

And that was that!

The smiling Australian told me that all the documents required would be sent to my home address, the Australian government would pay my fare and that I didn't even have to pay the ten pounds that most immigrants had to pay toward the transport charge as I would be underage, whatever that meant, at the time of travel.

I walked back to work in a bit of a daze not even noticing the rain just wondering what had hit me. I mean, I liked my job, I earned a reasonable salary, I had friends and family in Cardiff, and I didn't even know where Australia was. Much less how I was going to get there and what to expect when I arrived!

I didn't tell anyone what I had done, the fact was that to some extent, even I wasn't sure what had just happened, but that I had been offered a job in some far-off place where we had in the past deported criminals and as far as I was then aware, we could still be deporting them! I decided to think about things a lot more before saying a word to anyone.

For a few days, I played around in my head with the idea unsure if I really wanted to go or not. Some of my thoughts seemed quite pleasant whilst others completely turned me off the idea. Finally, I decided the time had come to tell a few friends and gauge their reaction. For the most part, that was like talking to a plant of wood. Their first question was why I wanted to go there. My answer was equally daft when I replied that I didn't know. The conversation then changed to more academic content as we discussed the actual location of Australia and was it nearer to the UK than America, Canada or even New Zealand? To be quite honest, the only reason we could name these countries was because they all kept advertising for Brits to leave the rain and the slag heaps behind and join them whilst making a new life for themselves in paradise. It was just luck that Australia had managed to get to me first, otherwise, this book may have been about my trials and tribulations in Canada!

It didn't take long before I received a few documents from Australia House which at the time was located on the Strand in London. They officially informed me that I had been accepted by this great commonwealth nation, and that I would need to stay there for a minimum of two years after which, should I wish to return to the UK, I was free to do so. Should I leave before the two years had expired, I was expected to pay not only my return fare but to also reimburse the Australian government for my fare over there. I would not require a passport for travel as I would be issued an identity card that was valid for a single journey only between the two countries. One document that stood out was to be signed by my parent or guardian and returned as soon as possible so that the Australians could arrange a departure date.

That was it! I decided that I was going and as I had to get the document signed, I had better tell my parents of my plans.

One lunchtime, soon after receiving the documents, I managed to get my mother and father together with the express intention of informing them that I was leaving. This would be a piece of cake, after all, with all the arguments and problems we were having, they would probably go upstairs and pack my bags for me. I may even get a lift on the crossbar of my father's bike to the railway station!

All three of us sat around the kitchen table when I made my big announcement.

"I'm going to Australia!" I told them. They both looked at me with some surprise showing on their faces before my father spoke.

"You're mad," he said and continued eating his lunch.

"Me mad? Are you looking in the mirror or something? Anyway, mad, or not, I am going!" I gave him a false, sickly grin.

"And how do you propose to get there?" He smirked, showing his all-knowing look.

"Well, I'm not going to walk, am I? The Australian government will pay my fare!"

With a look of almost contempt on his face, he sneered, "They'd never accept you anyway!"

It was my turn to scoff as I shot back at him, "A fat lot you know, they already have!"

With that, I produced the document that I needed him to sign, proving that I had my parents' permission to travel. I gleefully flashed it in front of him and told him that I just required his signature.

"No!" He flatly replied with a straight face, "I'm not signing anything, and you're not going!"

"Not signing it, why? Still learning to write, are you?" I yelled back at him.

Another row broke out during which I appealed to my mother to intervene on my behalf the appeal didn't seem to work so, finally, I yelled at him, "Don't sign it. I'll sign for you!" With that, I snatched the paper back.

"Sign it for him, Jim," my mother said in a quiet voice, "sign it and let him go." His face changed, and looking almost human, he nodded his head in defeat. I handed the paper back to him and he briefly glanced at it.

"If you go there, you may never see us again," he said. "We both may die before you come back!" Looking as serious as I could manage, I nodded my head. With all the arguments and problems, we were having he was going to miss me? No way, and in any case, he would still be able to argue with my mother after I had left!

The document signed and sent off things got incredibly quiet around the house. No arguments or problems, just peace at last. To this day, I still do not understand how he could hate me for most of my life and yet, when I was leaving, take another approach. I think it was all show, his way of showing my mother that deep down he was a good, caring father. She may have believed it, but I didn't. In the back of my mind, I knew that he was always planning or scheming something.

The departure date was finally confirmed by Australia House, leaving me with about a month to make complete preparations. I gave one week's notice to the Western Welsh, informed the taxman that I was leaving (I had been told that I could get a tax rebate) and paid a final visit to all my relations to say goodbye. As I had been expecting to go by boat (flying was only for the rich in 1963), the Australian government had surprised me by arranging for me to fly from London, Heathrow all the way to Melbourne, Australia (wherever that was) and my sister had press-ganged my brother-in-law to travel on an overnight bus with me to London. She had a young baby and was unable to travel herself, so it would be just me and her husband, something that I relished, as the idea of going alone did not impress me.

A few days before the arranged travel date I had my new suitcase packed and again checked my money. With my pay from the Western Welsh and my tax rebate, I had a total of forty-six pounds in total which I kept in a small wooden box in my wardrobe. It was not a lot of money, but it was all that I could put together.

I checked the total every morning and evening until the day before I was leaving when, to my horror, instead of forty-six pounds, the total in the box was only twenty-three. Rushing downstairs, I told my mother of the missing money. She told me that I must have made a mistake but that was not possible; I'd checked it too many times!

There were only three of us living in the house at that time, my mother, father, and me. I know she did not take it and I know that I didn't, but I also now knew who was responsible for other things that had previously disappeared!

Finally, the time had arrived to leave the comparative safety of Cardiff and travel into the great unknown. As it was a Sunday night, my parents had left my baby brother with the aunt and had left the house to go to the Cathay's Liberal Club with a promise to meet me at the bus station to say farewell. Their son might be leaving for the other side of the world, but the club was far more important than that.

I went upstairs for the last time to say goodbye to my bedroom and, picking up my suitcase, went back down again, kissed my aunt and my baby brother on the cheek and without looking back, I headed to Cardiff Bus Station.

My brother-in-law was waiting when I arrived and, much to my surprise, so were many aunts and uncles plus a few of my old mates from the bus company. My mother and father arrived straight from the club, and after everyone said their goodbyes, my brother-in-law and I boarded the bus and with a purr of the engine, we started out toward London.

It was a long, boring journey. There were no motorways in those days, and the journey seemed to go on forever. We had a twenty-minute stop at the ancient town of Bath and then continued with the never-ending jerking of the bus until we arrived at Victoria Coach Station the following morning.

From there, we travelled across London and went to the Australian Consulate in the Strand where, after telling them my name, they gave me a dark brown ID card and a ticket to travel on a Qantas Airlines flight to Sydney with a second ticket to change planes there and fly again to Melbourne. A useful piece of advice was that if we went to the BOAC terminal in central London I could check in my suitcase and say goodbye to it until I arrived in Melbourne. We took their advice and after checking it in, we were told that if we returned later, we could then board the BOAC bus that would take us directly to the terminal at the airport.

Heathrow in those days was small with only two terminals: The Queens Building and Terminal One. But it was still exciting, especially to people who had never visited an airport before much less travelled on a plane. From the observation deck, we could see over the parking apron on which were parked many propeller-driven aircraft and one of the latest jet-propelled planes. Painted all over it were the words 'Qantas Australia' and I knew then that I would be travelling on the world's biggest plane—the Boeing 707. I was still feeling scared as I had no idea what I was letting myself in for!

Chapter Six

I had passed the point of no return; my brother-in-law had left to return to Cardiff, and I was completely alone, no family or friends to take advice from so, from this moment on, I would be on a wing and a prayer.

In those days, there was no real immigration control and no need for security. Each passenger walked to a single booth that serviced the whole terminal, you showed your passport (or in my case ID card) and your ticket and you were ready to board your flight. On the other side of what passed for immigration was a small lounge with three or four gates leading off it. Each gate had a small slope leading away and at the bottom of these slopes, you would either walk or catch a bus to your aircraft.

Standing amongst a small group of people, I had very little idea of what would happen next however, I had reverted to my life-long philosophy: 'If in doubt, put a brave face on.' It seemed to work and as far as I was aware, I was passing off as being a normal passenger who had been flying almost every day and for whom all this was a perfectly normal part of life. In truth, I was scared stiff!

Reading an airport magazine, I was surprised to learn that the plane I was going to travel on was the only jet plane in service in the entire world and had replaced the Comet aircraft which, although it was the first jet to fly, had been taken out of service after three years due to some engineering problems, that must have been printed to give passengers some extra confidence.

The flight was called, and slowly, with a large group of people I walked out of the gate onto the tarmac and up a set of aircraft steps onto the plane. Stepping inside and waiting for my eyes to adjust to the semi-darkness, I could see that there were six seats in each row, three on either side of the aisle, and together they seemed to stretch back as far as the eye could see!

The plane seated around 140 passengers but, for a first-time flyer, it looked large! I was shown to a window seat halfway down the jet and was soon joined by two other men, one who sat in the middle seat and the other in the aisle. They were both aged about forty and wished me a good afternoon as they began to get comfortable for what would be a forty-six-hour journey to Sydney plus an additional two hours from there to Melbourne.

Although in 1963, flights were a great deal slower than today's modern aircraft, they were certainly a lot more comfortable. My seat was wide with lots of legroom and enough side space for me and my two travelling companions to sit with plenty of room to move around. Entertainment on planes was unheard of in those days, but at the back of the seat in front of me was a foldaway tray and small storage compartment with a magazine and safety card much like on today's aircraft. A small pillow was provided for each passenger to use as a headrest and on which to try and sleep during the two nights of our adventure.

With the four engines roaring, we taxied and started a long run until, just when I thought we would never take off we were suddenly airborne and climbing to our cruising height. Once the plane levelled out, the cabin stewardesses did not waste a moment before making themselves busy pushing their drink trolleys along the aisle and offering each passenger a large choice of free drinks and snacks. I asked for a can of beer which helped me to relax and feel quite relieved that we had not suffered any engineering problems on take-off.

With the drinks that were offered each passenger received a finely printed Qantas menu that listed the choice of food that would be available on this, the first leg of our journey. Another document was a route map of the entire forty-six-hour flight and for the first time since I started my journey, I discovered that we would, in all, be making eight stops. Rome would be our first port of call followed by Tehran, New Delhi, Bangkok, Singapore, Jakarta, Darwin and finally Sydney. It appeared to me that no one was in much of a hurry to get to Sydney as at each stop-over, the aircraft would be on the ground for up to two and a half hours so that it could be refuelled and serviced.

We were also given free postcards, some with a photo of the aircraft on one side and others that showed historical or tourist sites of interest to passengers in each of the countries we were, however briefly, about to visit. As they had space for writing an address and attaching a postage stamp, I decided that if the postage wasn't too expensive, I would send a card to my parents and my sister and her family from every stop, as written proof that I had been there.

Apart from buying soft drinks the sending of the postcards occupied a large portion of my time whilst we were on the ground. In the message space, I simply wrote the name of the city I was in.

The food served on the aircraft was abundant and tasty, much better than the food I had been used to at home. A choice of meals from the menu was available and then served on a large tray which was continually added to with the arrival of further courses. Wines and all manner of drinks were constantly refilled and smoking between courses was not only allowed but actively encouraged. Cigarettes or cigars were the order of the day when flying in those days and being a confirmed smoker, I willingly joined in. It must have been disappointing for pipe smokers though, as they were banned from lighting up.

After we landed in Rome, I become a little more relaxed. After all, I was now an international traveller and I was sure that the metal object in which we were flying could take off, land and stay in the air when it was required to do so.

On the ground, I had posted my cards taken from the aircraft as planned and was sitting down smoking a cigarette when I was joined by the two men who sat next to me on the plane. After exchanging names, we started a conversation.

"Where are you travelling to?"

"Sydney, well actually, I'm really going to Melbourne," I replied.

"So, are we, are you going there to work on the railway?"

"Yes, but I've got no idea of what I'm supposed to be doing after I arrive." They both laughed.

"Don't worry, we have no idea either." With another laugh, the ice had been broken and all three of us were now travelling companions!

Together, we slowly travelled halfway around the world and at each port of call, I dutifully mailed my postcards home, hoping, but never sure, if they would be delivered or if the postage money would just be stolen and placed in someone's pocket. This new adventure seemed to be working out quite well; my new friends helping me find the post office at each airport and lots of jokes and silly comments passing between the three of us. At one of the stop-overs I decided to buy duty-free cigarettes and purchased a carton of '555 State Express'. I'd never heard of the brand before but as they were made in America and were packed in little tins as opposed to the normal packaging, they seemed to me to be just the sort of thing an international traveller would smoke! I even kept the packaging as a souvenir long after the cigarettes had been used up.

We were all slowly feeling more and more exhausted as we finally made landfall in Australia. Darwin, to be precise! I later found out that it was a small outback town located in Australia's Northern Territory, but my first view of the place only confirmed that it had an airport that consisted of a series of wooden sheds and nothing much else.

As we disembarked from the aircraft, the other passengers and I all formed a queue, and each was in turn presented to a man seated behind a desk and looking very officious. Well, as officious as any Australian could look in 1963.

He was sporting a light brown uniform made of thin material and wearing shorts! Up until that time in my life I had never seen a grown man with hairy legs wearing shorts and I wondered, did he wear swimming trunks when his shorts were being washed? It all appeared very strange and laughable.

I was now at the head of the queue and the official asked for my ID and health card—just before I had left Cardiff, I had to go to the local hospital with a form sent to me by the Australian government and the hospital had injected me with a few types of vaccine and then issued me with a health card—anyway I digress. I duly handed both documents to the man. He looked at them, handed the ID card back to me and placed the health card in a small pile in front of him. That finished, I joined my two friends who were sitting on a bench in the large wooden hut.

After perhaps twenty minutes of sitting there a dilapidated loudspeaker system (probably a remnant of the Second World War) crackled into action and announced in an Aussie accent, "Will Brian Robson, please contact the desk of the medical officer?" My heart almost stopped; why me? Did I have the plague or something? Maybe it was something I had caught from travelling back and forth amongst all those Welsh slag heaps? I stood up and slowly made my way to the medical officer's desk, fearing the worst.

"I'm Brian Robson," I informed him whilst half expecting him to don a face mask.

"Oh, all right, blue," he replied, "look, it's about your medical card; did you get your injections done in a hospital?"

No, a veterinarian's surgery I thought but nodded my head in the positive.

"Oh, that's good because although they've put the vaccine number down, they seem to have forgotten to stamp the card."

"Did they really?" I replied, pretending to be interested but so tired that I could not have cared less.

"Yeah, but no problem, mate, we'll just have to jab you again; any problem with that?"

"No, no problem," I stammered, not relishing the thought of having more needles stuck in me whilst at the same time I promised myself to never trust the Cardiff Royal Infirmary again!

By now it was early morning and the sun had not yet started to rise, but with the vaccinations completed, I got back on the plane with the other passengers, and we took off yet again, heading in the general direction of Sydney, New South Wales. I couldn't help but wonder what was happening in 'Old' South Wales, but it would be sometime in the future before I found that out.

We had taken off again and been flying about an hour. The crew were serving a meal when the captain invited us to look out of the window and view our first Australian bushfire. It was nice of him to bother but I was so tired that I couldn't care less however, I managed to force myself. We were flying at 30,000 feet and were travelling over the fire for ten or fifteen minutes; it was massive. Funny people I thought, why doesn't someone bother to put it out? I did not realise at that time that it was located somewhere in the outback and that people on the ground probably didn't even know that the place was on fire. It was a while after this that I realised that Australians had a different culture and didn't quite see the world in the same light as their European counterparts.

"Ladies and Gentlemen, we are about to descend into Sydney (Kingsford Smith) Airport, will you please fasten your seatbelts, place your trays in an upright position and refrain from smoking until you have disembarked from the aircraft?" That was the crew telling us that finally, forty-six and a half hours after leaving London, the jet would make its landing at Sydney and we would disembark into a glorious Australian summer morning!

After landing we were met at the international arrivals by a man holding a sign that read 'Victorian Railway' and the three of us introduced ourselves and were welcomed by him to Australia. After the introductions were over, he informed us that he would be taking us to Sydney's second airport in a district known as Mascot where we had reservations to board a domestic flight to Melbourne. The three of us and our luggage were bundled into a small car and driven the short distance to the passenger terminal at the new Airport. As we arrived the aircraft was already boarding so we took our seats and the old Fokker Friendship turboprop plane humped and bumped down the runway and flew us on to our destination. This part of our journey was rather frightening, as the centre-cabin section of the aircraft swayed so much I thought that it would fall apart.

Two hours later, we were again met, this time at Essendon Airport, in Melbourne, and driven to the accommodation that had been arranged for us by the State Railway of Victoria. It needs to be said that since leaving Cardiff and up to the time I arrived here I had been travelling continuously for approximately fifty-nine hours and with, if any, truly little sleep. To say I was exhausted would have been an understatement. All I was looking forward to being something to eat and good sleep!

The accommodation supplied by the State Railway of Victoria was, to be perfectly honest, one of the biggest shocks of my nineteen years of living. Imagine a wild west town in an old black and white cowboy film, lots of wooden shacks, dirt roads, pools of dirty water and horses tied up to hitching posts—I lied about the horses and the hitching posts, but the rest of the place was exactly the same! There was muck everywhere. The toilet block was taken directly from the movie *Stalag 17* and there was a concrete wash-and-shower house, a canteen, and a large room with a television. The complete place housed around one hundred railway employees, all sleeping two to a basic room. My two travelling companions and I frequently shot a glance sideways at each other during the conducted tour and if we hadn't been so tired would we have burst out laughing at the conditions the Aussies expected us to live under.

My travelling companions were given a twin room to share, and I was ushered into a second room and told I would be sharing but that my roommate was currently at work. Not having met the guy, my first thoughts were that he could well stay at work for all I cared!

After the room allocation had been completed, we were shown into the canteen where a late lunch had been left for us. Our guide, who turned out to be the manager of the place, told us, before beating a hasty retreat, that he would meet us at 8 o'clock the next morning to take us to work. We were left alone, all looking a bit stunned as a plate of slop was placed on the table in front of each of us. Slop would have been a gourmet description for the concoction that was staring back at me from the plate. As far as I could tell it was a plate of liquefied grease with a few unidentifiable objects floating around in it. All three of us looked at each other simultaneously before pushing the plates away, getting up from the table and quickly returning to one of the rooms we had been allocated to and sitting on a bed.

"What the hell is this supposed to be?" one of my companions blurted out.

"I'm not staying here!" I chipped in quickly.

My second companion who was more restrained than both of us countered with, "Let's not jump to conclusions; we've just arrived; we are exhausted, and quite frankly, we have no idea where we are or where else to go. Why don't we all get some sleep and discuss the whole thing later?"

We all agreed about the sleep, and as I stood up to make my way to my room, I mumbled, half to myself, "Well, I'm still not staying here!"

In whatever way, my Australian adventure had begun!

Chapter Seven

I slept the rest of that day and all the following night, waking up around five the next morning. Not daring to return to the canteen in case the slop was still waiting there to attack me, I went to the toilet block, took a shower and ended up knocking at the door of my travelling companions' room.

They were both wide awake, and after being invited in, I sat on the edge of a bed and was intrigued to hear what conclusions they had both arrived at. The outcome of the brief conversation was that we should all attend the first day of work and see what wonders awaited us. It was also agreed that we had no option other than to stay there in the hostel, at least for a while, as at that stage, none of us had any idea of how to find another place to live—and in my case not much money to spend on doing so. Going along with the railway's plans for us, even if nothing else would mean that we would be paid and that anything else they offered couldn't be much worse than the food and accommodation that had already been given and who knew, perhaps things would improve after we found our feet and our way around.

Later we were collected by the manager and taken to one of the main railway offices in Melbourne, located above Flinders Street Railway Station. The training school was on the 3rd floor and we were shown around and introduced to the training staff. The station seemed to restore some form of normality as it seemed to be just like any other railway station anywhere in the world. It was big and had many platforms with trains arriving and departing by the minute. It looked as though thousands of people were either boarding or disembarking from the trains and with others just milling around passing the time whilst they waited for their journey to start. Maybe this whole nightmare was not quite as bad as it had at first appeared to be!

The school also seemed normal. It had three or four classrooms, all teaching different subjects related to working on the railway.

We eventually sat down in our classroom with the other twenty or so students who had joined us. Our instructor informed everyone that we would be attending each day for the week and at the end of that time would have to sit a test. Subject to passing it, we would be given a uniform and allocated a railway station where we would be expected to work. If we failed the test, we would have to take the course over again. The general purpose of the study, apart from showing us the layout of the railway and our duties, was to help us learn as many stations as possible on each of the railway lines in addition to where all these lines terminated. We would even practice when and how to wave a red or green flag at a train, how to blow a whistle and say boo to the train driver.

A good thing about that first morning was the discovery of the railway canteen. Located in the basement of the building, it served real food and drinks, none of which looked or tasted like yesterday's slop. We had to pay for what we ordered as it was not free as it was in the bunker where we existed and were expected to live—actually, as we learned later, that wasn't free either as a sum of money would be deducted each week from our wages to pay for our keep.

The school instructor was an old boy who looked as if he was about to retire, but he was quite fun and mainly due to his being a smoker himself gave us regular smoke breaks throughout the day. He made us laugh with trying to memorise the names of the stations where trains terminated. Although there were seven train lines in all, the funniest-sounding terminal was Dandenong, or it seemed to be at the time, and we derived many new silly pronunciations involving the place name.

Gradually, the members of the class got to know each other, and I and my travelling companions were surprised to learn that we were the only three immigrants studying on that course. The other class members were all born in Australia and so had a slight advantage over us in that most knew the geographical layout of Melbourne and hence the railway lines and routes. They also didn't seem to find some of the district names funny, whereas we were in hysterics and even had some difficulty pronouncing them.

We had, by now, got into a routine of eating in the railway station canteen before returning home each evening so we could avoid the poison that they served up back in the hostel. One evening, a boy about the same age as me and who was studying in our class joined us at our table.

"You fellas settling in?" he asked in his broad Aussie accent.

"Yeah, I suppose so," I answered.

"Where do you come from?"

"UK," said one of my travel companions, "you?"

"Waverley, I live with Mum and Dad!"

"That's a long way to travel every day," I chipped in, knowing that it was the terminal station of one of the train lines.

"No." He laughed. "I stay at my uncle's near here while I do the course. I'll go back home when I've finished the training."

"Lucky you; we stay in the sheds they call a hostel," I pulled a face when I said it.

"No good?"

"Good? It's so posh even the rats wear carpet slippers!" The boy looked at me, then at the others, and we all burst out laughing. "It's total crap!"

"Why don't you find somewhere else to live?" he asked us.

I looked at him as if he were daft. "Because all we know of bloody Australia is the way to class, this canteen and the way back to the hostel."

"You want a tour of the city?"

"When?" I quickly asked him.

"Now, if you want!"

Nodding our heads, we hurriedly finished our meal and left on a walking tour of the central district of Melbourne. I was surprised at how wide the roads were and to see that all the main thoroughfares had dual tram lines with single decker trams running on them. The buildings were tall and very Victorian looking. A few pubs were dotted here and there, and I noticed that they were all closed. When I asked the boy why, looking confused, he said, "Well, it's 6 p.m."

"So, what's that got to do with anything?"

"All the pubs close at 6 p.m.; it's the law!"

"I bet they're closed on Sundays too?"

"How'd you know that?" he asked.

"I just guessed," I replied, remembering 'Old South Wales' and the Rhondda Valley.

We walked for about an hour around the centre of Melbourne and ended up back where we had started at Flinders Street Railway Station. Going up to the school and whilst I was collecting my belongings, the boy asked if I was going back to the hostel, and on hearing 'yes', he suggested that we might like to play a game of snooker in the staff snooker hall that was located next to the canteen before we went back. I jumped at the chance, not because I was any good or even really liked playing the game but rather as it would delay my return to the dreaded huts, we called home.

The snooker hall was large with about ten tables, and we all selected our cues and were allocated a table. I jokingly asked the boy where to install the batteries and taking me seriously, he mumbled to himself something about bloody Poms did not even understand the game. Continuing to play around with him, I said I had no idea of how to set the balls up, and so, whilst explaining the rules to me, he proceeded to arrange the table and I suggested that just to be sure I understood the game, he had better take the first shot whilst I watched him.

He took the break and scattered the balls all around the table, then motioned to me to take my shot. I looked around the table, and right at the far end and roughly in the centre of the width of the table was a solitary red ball. I, whilst keeping a straight face, double-checked with him that I should try to pocket that ball. With a slight shrug of his shoulders, he said that it was up to me so taking careful aim, I hit the white which hit the red at a fast pace and a perfect angle. The red ball shot into the top left-hand pocket and the white ball dribbled on up the table only to stop inches behind the black ball. Taking careful aim, I pocketed the black into the top right-hand pocket, and whilst he retrieved the ball, I stood there triumphantly with a big grin on my face! He looked astonished as, with a serious face, I said, "Like that?"

"I thought that you'd never played before?" He gasped.

"Silly bloody Aussie, the bloody Poms invented the game, so I guess I must have!" I answered.

We both started laughing, but I must admit they were probably the only two balls I sunk in the whole game!

Chapter Eight

Within a few days of our snooker evening, we had finished the course, passed the tests and were taken by train to Spencer Street Railway Station, Melbourne's departure point for interstate trains. There, we were issued identity cards and new uniforms. Dark blue in colour, they were made of quite a good material and partially resembled a lounge suit with the addition of black buttons and a peaked cap. Although off the rack, we were checked and measured for size, and we all looked rather dapper in them.

Walking the distance back to Flinders Street we passed a building with a brass plate attached to the side of the door frame. It read: 'Office of the British Consulate'. I instinctively knew that I had some business there and made a mental note of the address.

On reaching Flinders Street, we went to our classroom and all sat down wearing our new uniforms. The instructor then allocated the name of the station where we would need to report for work. I was to be working at a station called 'Ascot' on the northern line, and I was told to report to the station master at the place the following Monday morning. We were all then congratulated on knowing the difference between red and green signal flags, said goodbye to each other and made our way out of the building. When we reached the main road, I excused myself from my two travel companions and told them that I would meet them at the hostel later.

Immediately upon leaving them I found a telephone booth, phoned the operator, and asked for the number of the 'British Consulate in Melbourne'. She gave me the number which I dialled and was put through to a young lady with the unbelievable name of Miss Cardiff! She listened to what I had to say before suggesting that I go and meet with her the following morning.

The next day being Saturday, I was up early and making my way to the building on which I had seen the 'British Consulate' plaque. After being shown into a nicely furnished office, I was seated on a sofa next to the aptly named Miss

Cardiff and was offered a cup of coffee to which I answered yes. She was smiling at me as I told her about the accommodation and where they could stick Australia.

"So how long have you been here, Brian?" she smiled as she asked the question.

"About eight days, and that's eight days too long!" I mumbled back.

"Do you think that you've given it a fair try?"

"A fair try, are you joking?" I asked. "Have they given me a fair try? I'm living in a stinking hole; no one has even offered any help, asked if I have any problems, or shown us around the place—they can stick it!"

"I see your point and I understand you want to leave but, in all honesty, we have no authority to send you home. That would be up to the immigration department of the Australian government in Canberra, and that's a long way away! I would suggest that you calm down a bit and slowly think things out; after all, you just might begin to like it here!"

"I won't like it here. I don't want to like it here, my mind is made up, and I'm going home!" I replied.

"Well look, for the time being you're very welcome to come here and see me at any time you wish. We can chat, have a cup of coffee or you can read the British newspapers and at least keep in touch with the UK in that way."

"I don't want to chat, and I don't like coffee," I almost growled back, "I want to go home!"

I could see that I was wasting my time and getting nowhere so, as politely as I could, I thanked her for her time and promptly left the office. I was even angrier now as not only was I stuck in Australia, but the British government had no intention of even trying to help me get back home.

The next day, being Sunday and the last day before I was due to report to the station where I was going to work, I decided to try and wash some clothes. I'd never even tried to do that before and so I took a bundle to the concrete washhouse and made a half-hearted attempt to get them clean. When they all looked clean enough to me, I went back to my room and, after hanging them up to dry, went to visit my travel companions who were looking as depressed as I felt. All three of us were starting work the next day, but they, being more fortunate than me, were both working at the same station and so had each other for company. We chatted about what we would be doing if we were still in the UK and then I left them to go to bed, as we had to get up early the next day.

Monday morning started with a walk to Flinders Street and then a train to travel the six kilometres to my new place of work.

Ascot Railway Station consisted of a one up and one down platform with two sets of railway tracks running between them. I arrived just before 8 o'clock and after spending a few minutes just looking around the place I crossed both tracks on foot and reported to an office where the sign read 'Station Master'. The front section of the building was a ticket office with a wall dividing it from a rear office containing just a desk and two chairs. The only person visible to the naked eye was a young guy standing in the ticket office section and selling the occasional ticket. I waited until he had finished playing with his ticket machine before I approached him; then I introduced myself.

"Morning, my name's Brian, and I'm supposed to meet the station master at 8 o'clock," I said.

"You're the new guy, right?" he asked.

"Yeah, you the station master?"

"Nope, no such luck, I just do every other job around here!"

"So, where's the boss man?"

"You won't see him until later this afternoon, he opens up in the morning, then disappears until later in the day!"

"What am I supposed to do then?" I asked.

"Up to you really, but if you want, I'll sell the tickets and you dispatch the trains?" He grinned at me.

"From where you want me to dispatch them?"

"It's up to you really, but both platforms if you can manage it? Just ignore any timetable, wave a flag and blow your whistle whenever you remember to do it!" His grin got even bigger, and it was obvious that he couldn't care less what I did.

So, I spent my first working day on Victorian Railways jumping down and climbing up platforms, running across rail lines whilst in between all the running around I was waving a green flag and blowing my bloody whistle at any train that bothered to stop! I had no idea where the trains were coming from or going to or how many people got on or got off or who had a ticket or who didn't!

Sometime later in the day, the guy from the ticket office joined me and asked if I wanted to go with him for a bite to eat? I asked him who would look after the station whilst we were gone, and he said that the devil himself could take care of it. The train guards, seeing that no one was on the platform, would signal the driver to get going and as for people wanting to buy tickets, well, they could bloody well pay the fare when they reached their destination!

We both walked out of the station and into a small milk bar where we both ordered something to eat and drink, we sat down before the guy spoke to me again, "How much did you collect?"

"Collect? What are you talking about?"

"Collected money – the money from the passengers who arrived without tickets?"

"I didn't collect anything, I just did what you told me to do, wave the green flag and blow the bloody whistle. I never went anywhere near the exit or ticket office on platform two, and you were stuck in the ticket office on platform one?"

Nodding his head, he then went on to tell me about the fiddle that was used at many of the Victoria Railway's many stations. Apparently, lots of passengers boarded trains without buying tickets, and so it was the job of the station assistants to stand at the exit checking those who have paid and those that hadn't. The secret, so I was informed, was to hold the queue up by double-checking the first few passengers' tickets twice over. Other people waiting in the now-forming queue would get impatient and start to walk past whilst, at the same time, pushing the money owed for the fare into your hand. Station assistants were then supposed to take the money into the ticket office and issue tickets to the value of the money collected.

I told him that I knew about this as I had been told during my training period, he then said that I didn't know about the big secret!

"What big secret?" I asked.

"Don't bother to issue any frigging tickets. The money collected is used to pay for food and drinks and is shared by you, me and the boss. Is that okay with you?"

I told him that was up to him and the station master and that as for me, a mere beginner, I would do exactly as I was told!

I divided the rest of the day between blowing whistles, waving my green flag, and collecting money to pay for our meal breaks!

After a hard and boring day running Victoria's Railways, I arrived back to my room only to find a note on my bed. It was from my two travel companions and it informed me that they had not gone to work that day but had, in fact, moved out of the hostel and found a better job. They signed off by telling me that they would be in touch with me again as soon as possible.

That really made my day whilst I had been blowing my whistle, those two had buggered off without taking me with them!

Chapter Nine

The days turned into a few boring weeks, and my time was equally shared between attending the most boring job in the world and hanging around in the world's worst accommodation. Ninety per cent of my working day was spent on my own blowing whistles at trains which I hoped that I would never see again but that I knew would return to the station every few hours or so. I often wished that I could swap my whistle for one that made a noise that resembled someone passing wind. That would make a good send-off for both the train and its passengers!

The evenings in the hostel were just as bad and were spent either laying on my bed and dreaming that I was back in Cardiff or watching Australian television programmes, that were produced on a very low budget and interceded with very old programmes from the UK and watched on the television in the hostel's television room.

The television room was a sight to behold! Around thirty or forty old and near-retiring age employees would sit in a darkened room lit only by the flickering screen of the black and white television set. Seating was provided by hard wooden benches that, after ten minutes, would give you both back and bum ache, and to top it all off, everyone smoked!

Now, as I said before I was a regular smoker but even, I couldn't stand the amount of smoke that was produced in that room and had to take an outside breath of fresh air at regular intervals. After gulping down the fresh air I would return to the room to find that someone had stolen my seat and so began the search for a new place to sit. I would proceed with arms flaying around, trying to force a path through the cigarette smoke that was so thick that many times I could not even see the television screen!

Most of the residents of the hostel seemed to me as though they were past retirement age; they spoke with an almost non-comprehensible Aussie accent and carried a bottle of alcohol around with them just about everywhere they went.

However, my roommate was an exception to the rest of them as he never seemed to be there. I had met him just once after my arrival, and we had said a brief hello. I never saw him again, and he didn't even pop in from time to time to collect clean clothing. I was told that he worked on the interstate trains and that he would spend weeks away. The longer he was away was okay with me as I didn't fancy sharing a room, not even with an interstate worker.

One evening when I was laying on my bed, dreaming of the Top Rank back in Cardiff there was a knock on the door. Getting up off the bed, I opened it, and low and behold, my two ex-travel companions were standing there, grinning at me! Leaving the door open for them to come in, I walked back to my bed and sat down.

"What are you two doing here?" I asked.

"We've come to collect you" was the reply.

"What do you mean—to collect me? You just disappeared, and now you want to collect me, collect me for what?"

"Are you still pissed off with Australia?"

"Of course, I am, and getting more and more pissed off by the day!"

"Well, we've come back to give you some help."

"Help me? You couldn't help yourselves!" I said whilst sounding completely disinterested in anything else they had to say.

The pair started to explain that the reason they had left was that on the morning they were due to start work on the railway, someone had told them that General Motors, based in Dandenong (of all places), was looking for people to work in its factory. They had immediately caught a train to the place, applied and been given jobs before returning to the hostel, gathered their stuff together, rented a small room near the factory and starting work!

"Did you give your notice in here?" I asked for no apparent reason.

"Bugger them, what help did they give us, unless you can call a crap job and this place help?"

I had to nod my head in agreement with that before I asked them for more details of this so-called job and they told me that it was shift work, assembling fridges. Oh, and the money was much better than the railways. If I wanted to work there, I could stay with them until I had enough money to rent my own room and that if I was quick the factory still had more vacancies.

That was it, it didn't take much to convince me, and so without as much as a goodbye to the hostel I packed my suitcase and left the place with my friends.

We travelled thirty-six miles to Dandenong, using my ID card to board the train and avoid the fare. When we arrived at our destination and tried to exit the station, I showed the station assistant my pass and he asked about my friends' tickets? With a big grin, I answered him, "stuff off and pay for your own meal breaks!" We then walked out of the station, laughing.

My friends' room was part of a prefabricated building built along with a few other prefabs erected in the back garden of the landlord's house. This was quite a common way for the Aussies to make extra money. A wooden frame covered on both the inside and outside with some sort of gypsum board looked quite respectable and could be divided with partitions into separate rooms. The room they had rented was quite small but had two sets of bunk beds, a small table, a few chairs and its own private bathroom. It was the private bathroom that placed it into the luxury class as most lettings had only one or two bathrooms shared between as many rooms as the owners could fit into the buildings. Outside of the room, there was a grass lawn with some trees and a few wooden tables and benches dotted around, which made for quite a relaxing area and that was one hundred per cent better than the railway hostel.

Immediately I saw the place, I knew that I was going to like living there, and I quickly made plans to first get the job and then to rent my own room. My place would ideally be near to my friends' place so I would also have some company whenever I wanted it. The three of us had a small meal and then settled down for the night. I wanted to be completely refreshed to go to the factory the next day.

Dawn broke and I was up, showered and dressed before either of my colleagues had even woken up. This was a big day for me; a new job which hopefully, I would fit into quite well, plus a new place (even if it were only on a temporary basis) where I would like living. For the upcoming interview, I wore a tie which, as my brother-in-law had taught me sometime before, I had tied in a Windsor knot as it looked much more business-like.

My friends woke up and got themselves ready to show me where the factory was located. They had breakfast, but I was too hyped up to eat. I could hardly wait for them to finish eating and get to the place. Finally, after what had seemed like an eternity, they were ready, and we set off on the short walk.

When we arrived at the factory gates, my friends left me to make my own way to the administrative offices and to ask for an interview. With a big smile, I asked the girl at the front desk if they had any vacancies and she confirmed that they had. She asked me to take a seat for a moment.

After a short time, I was ushered into an office and given an application form which I duly completed in my best handwriting. I had no sooner completed it when a man entered the room, introduced himself and started reading my application. We were both smiling as he asked me a few questions; where did I come from, how long had I been in Australia, where did I live? Suddenly, he stopped smiling, and I intuitively knew something was wrong.

"Brian, how old are you?" he asked.

"Nineteen," I replied with a smile. His face looked profoundly serious.

"I'm really sorry," he said, "the only positions we have are on shift work and our company rules state that you have to be at least twenty years old before we can offer you a place!"

My smile quickly faded as I felt that I was falling through the floor. My new job, my new accommodation, my new life, it was all quickly disappearing.

"Please," I almost begged him, "I'll be twenty in about nine months!" He slowly, almost sorrowfully, shook his head.

"I really can't help you, I'm so sorry!"

With that, we shook hands and I walked back to the factory gates and to my friends who were still waiting there. Almost in tears, I told them what had happened. They were as shocked as I was but tried to cheer me up by telling me that there were loads of other factories around the area.

"Yeah," I answered, feeling completely helpless, "God, I hate this country!"

As we walked back to the rented room, I felt more depressed than ever. I'd never been refused a job before and now? Just because of my age? What a crap country Australia was! I could work better than anyone. I wasn't afraid to work, went on time—well, mostly and didn't ask for much. Bugger General Motors, they made crap cars and they're not even Australian anyway! As for their fridges, they could stick them. I would never ever buy a General Motors Fridge again! The thought didn't cross my mind that I had never bought any brand of fridge in my life before, never mind a General Motors one!

Later that day, my friends both went off to work and I was left alone in the rented room. I had got over my bout of depression and a positive side began to creep back into my attitude.

I was still dressed for an interview so why not go out now and look for a job? That's what I did, I went out and walked for what seemed like miles, stopping off at every factory I came across, always the same answer, "Come back when you're twenty years old!" By now and feeling desperate I came across a name that I knew well, 'Gillette'. That was a name that I knew from the UK, so I walked into the building feeling sure that I could get a job with them. Brimming with confidence, I walked up to the reception and asked for the tenth time that day if they had any vacancies?

"Where were you born?" the receptionist asked.

"Cardiff, in Wales," I confidently replied.

"Sorry, we don't employ foreigners," she mumbled.

"I'm not a foreigner, I'm British," I said before realising what a stupid answer that was. "You mean you only employ Australians?" I asked sheepishly.

"Yeah." She grinned back.

"Australians with the ball and chain marks around their legs that came from Britain in the first place or the ones that are still on the run from the law?" I gave her my dirtiest look and stormed out.

Enough was enough! I'd tried many factories, and now I was a foreigner in a bloody country where apart from the aborigines so was everyone else! Bloody, flea-ridden Aussie gits, at least I wasn't deported after being convicted of getting up to no good, unlike their mothers and fathers. They should all still be locked up in the colonies to which they had been sent and not allowed to roam freely amongst law-abiding immigrants!

Immigrants. I was even beginning to hate that word as well as the country that recruited them and then didn't offer any help. From now on, they would all be classed by me as Aussie dogs, at least that's the way I thought just then!

Chapter Ten

The following day, I woke up with a start and joined my friends for breakfast. We chatted for a while before we discussed the possibilities of me getting a local job in a factory. I told them that I didn't think it would be possible or, at the very least, difficult due to my age; however, I had another idea that I wanted to try. To put my idea into practice, I had to go back into the city, and so using my rail ID card I travelled back to the centre of Melbourne. I got off the train at the now-familiar Flinders Street Station and went into a telephone booth. Phoning the operator, I asked her for an address and phone number. She looked it up for me, and as I left the booth, I threw the phone number away and briskly walked to the address I had been given.

I went into the building, walked to reception and asked if they had any vacancies? After being told that they had, I was asked to wait and was then taken to meet a personnel officer. Introductions were made before he started asking me the usual questions, such as where I came from, what work did I do back there and how I had arrived in Australia.

After chatting for about ten minutes and with my stressing many times my employment with the Western Welsh Bus Company, he asked if I would excuse him for a moment and he left the room. Returning just a few minutes later, he told me that they could offer me a job, but before they did, he wanted me to do him a small favour. Apparently, he had just spoken with the railway people on the phone, and they would like a chat with me. He felt that as they had flown me to Australia it was only fair that I do that, and then after meeting with them and if I still felt unhappy, I could come back to see him, and he would offer me a job with the Melbourne Tram Company. I grudgingly agreed and upon leaving his office once again, made my way back to Flinders Street Station.

Upon arriving I asked to speak to the guy whose name I had been given and who was expecting me and we both sat down in his office. He was quite pleasant and offered me a cup of tea. We sat in silence, drinking it and then like a know-all father he said, "You're not happy in Australia, right? Missing your friends?"

"Missing my country," I replied with a big smirk.

"What's the difference between here and the UK?"

"One is mine and the other is yours!" I sarcastically replied.

"Not quite so." He quickly offered. "I came here from the UK with my family about twenty years ago; it's okay when you get to know the place."

"I bet you never lived in a filthy hostel or worked at a crap railway station virtually on your own, did you?"

"No, you're right there, we were given a house, and I went to school," he said before smiling, "and you don't have to stay in the hostel forever either."

Then he went on about how long it had taken him to settle down when he first arrived and how much crap he had to put up with, but now, after twenty years, he would never go back to the UK to live.

"I miss the slag heaps and the rain!" I scoffed.

Laughing, he caught me by surprise when he asked me if I wanted a milkshake.

"A milkshake, how'd you do that, get a woman to do a dance and jump up and down? Anyway, I've never tried one!"

Telling me that I should have tried one by now and that apart from beer milkshakes were the national drink of Australia, he took me across the street, and going into a milk bar, he ordered one for each of us—with extra malt!

"What's malt?"

"Wait and see." He smiled.

Whilst we were drinking it, he went into a lecture about how many things were different between the UK and Australia and how a lot of things in Aussie were better. I didn't agree with him, but I had to admit the milkshake was good!

We both walked back to his office with him telling me how the railway really needed my expertise and how my flag-waving was wonderful, how I would still have to live in the hostel, but, if I saved my money, how I would soon be able to rent a place of my own. He had hooked me, and I found myself unwillingly agreeing with him, mainly due to the fact that over the past few days, I had been turned down over so many jobs but what about that crap railway station?

"You fancy working at Spencer Street?" he asked me.

"The interstate place, yes, I don't mind," I heard myself saying.

"It's yours for the taking if you want; you can start working there tomorrow?"

Leaving his office, I went back to Dandenong, packed my stuff and saying goodbye to my two friends—who I never saw again—moved back into the hostel, I had sold myself out for a milkshake with extra malt!

Chapter Eleven

Working at Spencer Street Railway Station meant I could walk to work from the hostel and didn't need as before to catch a train. The first day, I arrived on time, and after finding the required office, I signed on to say I was there. Asking the clerk what I should do, I was told to speak to the foreman, but no one seemed to know where he was or how to find him. So, I just went for a walk around the station.

This was Melbourne's main interstate terminal and the only place where you could catch a train to travel to other states within Australia. My uniform meant that I could go anywhere within the station and so, taking full advantage, I went on an unorganised tour. I checked out the platforms, having a good look at all the trains, boarded some of the carriages, sat in the first-class sections and generally had a good time.

After a few hours of doing absolutely nothing, I returned to the foreman's office and found him busy having lunch.

"Hi, I'm Brian," I said.

"Oh, hi, we've been expecting you, have you just arrived?"

"No, I've been here since eight this morning."

"Have you been busy?"

"Pretty much so," I lied, "what do you want me to do now?"

"Have your lunch first, then just carry on as this morning" was his answer.

I smiled and said okay then, after leaving his office, spent about 90 minutes in the canteen before checking the same platforms out as I had done earlier. Orders were orders and who was I to disagree!

This turned into a regular daily routine; sign on, check the platforms out, check the canteen, do the afternoon round and go home. No one had any idea what I was doing and although it was a complete waste of my time, at least they would be paying me for being there.

That was exactly what happened, at the end of the week, my pay packet was waiting for me in the foreman's office and, pretending to be overworked I duly collected what was mine. This gave me enough money to look for a place to rent, and so, buying the 'Melbourne Age' newspaper and scanning the classifieds I finally found a small room in the suburb of Footscray and moved out of the much-hated hostel.

The room was not exactly a palace, but it was much better than the accommodation supplied by my employer. Fairly small, it had a single bed, a sofa and a small dining table. An alcove leading off the room contained a kitchen counter, cooker, sink and the few kitchen utensils that I would need to prepare exotic meals for myself. The one drawback was that it was located about six miles from the station where I was working which meant that I was unable to do both the early and late shifts as I had no transport and trains were not running at the times, I needed them. Giving it some thought, I applied for a transfer to Footscray Station as from my accommodation, I would then be able to walk to work at all hours of the day and night.

As soon as I settled into my new room, I made myself comfortable by renting a television which was proudly placed in a spot next to the old fireplace in the room. I placed the one single chair in front of the set so after work I could return home, turn the TV on and sit there all evening until time for bed.

Going shopping, I bought basic foodstuffs that didn't require much cooking mainly because, if the truth were told, I had absolutely no idea of how to cook. My evening meal would always consist of Welsh rarebit (grilled cheese on toast) and, if I do say so myself, I became an expert at preparing it. Nobody ever complained about the quality of my cooking, possibly because I was always there alone!

One day when out shopping for bread and cheese, I picked up a packet of instant cake mixture, and after reading the back of the packet, I was rather pleased to see that I would only need to add a few eggs to have the perfect cake. A tin of carrots looked tempting, and I thought perhaps I would change my diet. I was just about to purchase the bread, cheese, cake mix and carrots when an old lady asked me why I was wasting my money on a tin of carrots and why I didn't buy fresh ones? The tin, she informed me, was four times the price! I told her that I couldn't buy fresh as I didn't know how to cook them. With a laugh, she said, you cook them the same as you would a tin, in a saucepan with some water! I put the carrots back on the shelf and just bought the other bits that I needed.

Back at work, I was finally given a job to do. The foreman noticed me checking the platforms and asked if I was free to help load a train full of mail. Thinking it would pass some time, I readily agreed and slowly made my way to the platform he mentioned. The interstate train was standing there, and on the platform were stacked up many sacks of mail surrounded by maybe eight or ten station assistants none of whom I had met before whilst performing my platform inspections. Taking our time, we slowly, so as not to break into a sweat, loaded the sacks into the guard's van and after the job was completed, everyone except one other kid and I went back to the canteen to have a break. As they left, I noticed a letter that must have fallen from one of the sacks lying on the platform. I picked it up and asked the kid what I was supposed to do with it. He replied that he didn't know but maybe look for an open sack and push it back in. We both boarded the train to look for a sack that was open and, as we did so, the train jerked and before we had time to jump off, started picking up speed and left the station. What the hell do we do now, I asked him, stuffing the now-not-so-important letter into my pocket?

The train was travelling quite fast, and after quickly glancing at the bags we had loaded, we realised it was bound for Sydney over six-hundred miles away.

"Do you think it will stop before it gets there?" I asked him.

"I've got no idea," he answered, giving me a worried frown.

"It had better, or we'll be stuck here all night," I shot back at him.

"You think that they'll pay us overtime for that?" We both laughed.

I was about to write a letter to my new home address leaving my newly-rented television set to my landlord for safekeeping when, to our relief, the train's brakes came on and it gradually stopped at a station. We both jumped off before it had completely stopped moving and then, after having to wait about half an hour for the next train, we caught a train back to Melbourne.

It was dark when we reached Spencer Street, so we both signed out and left the station to go home. As we left, now laughing and relieved that we had survived this tremendous ordeal, I discovered that the boy lived quite close to me, and so I invited him back for tea. He accepted my offer, and we made our way to my humble abode.

Taking off my uniform jacket and inviting him to do the same I discovered the letter that I had found earlier. I threw it on the table and we both went into the kitchen, I to prepare the food and he, to watch a chef at work and to learn the art of cooking.

Remembering the cake mix that I had bought a few days earlier I suggested that we have Welsh rarebit followed by some nice homemade cake. This seemed agreeable to both of us and so, after reading the cake instructions, I looked for the two eggs needed to add to the mix and show off my cooking skills. Unfortunately, I could only find one and being a much knowledgeable and by-now-experienced cook, I decided to go ahead with the cake anyway.

I mixed the egg and some milk with the powder till it formed a cream and then cleverly put it in a shallow baking tin before popping it into the oven.

Whilst it was baking, I made the rarebit and we sat down to eat. As we finished the cheese on toast, I could tell by the smell from the oven that baking was complete, and I gleefully invited my guest into the kitchen to view the result! The cake looked perfect, and I took it out of the baking tin and put it onto a plate. Picking up a large knife, I held it above the cake, with its pointed end about two inches from the top, and then, with a flourish, I stabbed the knife down.

Much to the surprise of both myself and my guest, the knife hit the surface of my newly-baked masterpiece and with a sound like a 'bong' bounced back up leaving the cake completely unmarked. As hard as I tried, I just could not cut into the sodding thing! It was as solid as a block of cement. We didn't eat cake that evening, and I began to understand that it's always a good idea if you want to cook something to follow all the instructions on the packet!

Chapter Twelve

Melbourne got quite cold in the winter months and sitting in my room during the evenings was quite chilly. Looking at the empty fireplace, I could imagine a blazing fire glowing and lighting up the room. It's surprising how, by letting your imagination run away with you, you can begin to feel warmer. I had no idea where to buy coal accept perhaps to write a letter home asking them to send me part of a slag heap, but as it would take at least six weeks for a letter to get there, I ruled that idea out.

A few days later, on my way home from work, I called into a local shop and discovered that although they didn't sell coal, they did sell charcoal to be used in garden barbequing. That would do the trick I thought and purchased a bag that weighed a few kilos.

As soon as I arrived back at my room, I went into the garden, and after using the outside toilet and taking a quick shower whilst the weather was still warm, I hunted around to find a few sticks that would help me make the fire go with a roar. Finding a small quantity of wood, I returned to the room with it.

Now I just needed some paper! I searched around but found nothing and was just about to give up when I came across the letter that I had picked up on the platform of Spencer Street Station the day we took our train journey and explored the state of Victoria. I ripped it open and was surprised that it contained a cheque book. Oh well, it was too late to return it now, so I ripped a few cheques out and after writing a few of them out for a million pounds each, I crumpled them up complete with the envelope that the book came in. I then decided that as money had no meaning, I place each in the fireplace and laid a few wooden sticks on top. Next, I opened the charcoal and gently placed some of it on top of the sticks. I lit the cheques, and very soon I had a roaring fire going, giving a new meaning to the phrase 'to burn money!' It was great, a warm room, television on and two rounds of cheese on toast, and I was set for the night. I even topped up the fire before I went to sleep that night but by the time I woke up in the morning, it had gone out and the room was as chilly as ever. Never mind, at least, with the fire going out, I had saved some of the charcoal to use the next time I needed a fire.

That cheque book and the million-pound cheques seemed to fascinate me; it was too late to return the book and the cheques had proved useful for lighting fires. It could prove useful for other things, and so carefully placing it in my inside pocket, I took it almost everywhere I went. It seemed to give me some security, maybe I didn't have much money, but I had more than most people had. I had my own cheque book and with it a status symbol.

By now, living in Australia had become a bit of a game! I took nothing seriously, didn't care about anything and all my spare time was spent pretending I was back in Cardiff. I still had Saturday and Sunday as holidays from work, but it was unlikely that I would make many friends as the Aussies were sports mad and the weekends were filled with sporting activities arranged for them. All sport was something that I avoided like the plague. Even back in my school days, I would write my own sick notes to get myself excused from participating in those activities. I didn't really drink much in those days, but pubs would have been a place to meet people except for the fact that they still closed at 6 o'clock in the evening and by the time I returned from work, it was too late. A bit of window shopping was generally okay as all the shops were open on Saturday mornings until twelve lunchtime and then they closed until Monday morning. Mind you, shopping or window shopping was not usually considered to be a good way to make friends or meet people.

One Saturday morning, bored and with nothing to do, I caught the train into the centre of the city and spent some time listlessly wandering around. I ended up in the lobby of a large hotel and started to look at all the expensive shops that one would expect to find even today in lobbies of such large places. One shop caught my eye and I casually strolled in to look around. It was a souvenir shop selling many products that were either made in Australia or made perhaps in Malaysia—as that country was the exporter of many consumer goods made in Asia at that time. The products seemed to be of good quality and the asking price reflected either that or the shop thought that all consumers were rich and a little crazy.

I spoke to the lady working in the shop and asked if the goods were made in Australia, and she, assuring me that they were, went off to deal with another customer. I started browsing the shelves and within a short time had selected about twenty or so items. Seeing that I might be a big customer she came over to help me both select the products and in taking them to the cash desk. I was not sure that I was going to buy them or if I was just wasting time and would tell her that I would come and collect them later the next day, but before I had a chance to say anything, she was ringing the goods up on the cash register; the total cost came to about thirty pounds.

Thirty pounds was quite a large sum of money in those days and as I only had about three pounds ten shillings in my pocket, the method of paying for them became a slight problem. My not having anywhere near enough money to pay the bill, I was suddenly hit with an inspiration. "Will you take a cheque?" I asked her. with a smile.

"Certainly, sir," she answered.

I quickly wrote out a worthless piece of paper and after she had put my purchases into three carrier bags, I slowly left the shop wishing her an exceptionally good day.

To say the least, I was both excited and elated over what I had just done and as I continued to walk the streets looking into shop windows I wondered if I could buy an air ticket home using the same method. I soon forgot that idea when I remembered that even if I could buy a ticket, I still didn't have a passport and as sure as hell was hot, no government would accept a worthless piece of paper!

After arriving back in my room, I placed my purchases on the bed and after deciding that I should gift-wrap them, I went to my local shop and bought some gift-wrapping paper. I managed to scrounge an old cardboard box from the shop owner before returning home, wrapping each one and placing the soon-to-become gifts inside the box. Later, I would post them to the UK.

Monday morning arrived, and I took the now-sealed-and-addressed box with me to work. I signed on and after going to the post office I sent the box off. On the way back, I bumped into the station foreman.

"I've been looking for you," he said.

"I've been really busy today," I replied with my sweetest smile.

"Well, your dream job's been confirmed, as from tomorrow you're transferred to Footscray Station!"

"Thanks!" I said with a genuine smile, beginning to wonder if I was going to miss the platforms and canteen of Spencer Street.

Chapter Thirteen

Footscray Station was located barely ten minutes' walk from where I was living making it quite easy for me to get to work. I guessed that would probably be the only benefit that would go with the position and that the job would be as tedious and boring as any other station on the Victorian Railway.

Footscray was a four-platform station which meant it served not only as a stopping-off point for those who lived in the area but also as a junction where the rail lines split, so it handled trains that travelled along two different lines on both outward and inward directions and with the inward line terminating at Flinders Street. All trains travelling north out of the city would stop there to pick up and drop passengers off. The place was much bigger than the two-platform station where I had worked and so should have other people working there. At least, I would get the chance to meet someone.

With a feeling of complete disinterest, I arrived on time for work and reported to the station manager in his office. After sitting down with him, he asked where else I had been working and, although I thought it none of his business, I mumbled Spencer Street. He went on about that station handling interstate traffic, whereas this one handled local traffic. I tried to look happy and interested in what he was saying, but in my mind, I was wondering what time would be good to clock-out!

I had learnt by now to virtually ignore what any so-called manager said, as if truth be told, they knew about as much as I did, which was extraordinarily little. I also wondered why he needed to tell me about Spencer Street as I had already worked at the place and if I didn't know what happened there by now then I never would. After he had finished babbling on about nothing, I was sent to help the station assistants who were supposedly working on platform number two.

Doing a soft-shoe shuffle by dragging my feet and stopping every few yards to look at and study the advertisements, I slowly, very slowly, made my way to the platform. All the platforms were located on a second level and so I climbed a flight of stairs imitating the steps of an incredibly old man and finally reaching the top of the second platform.

Whilst I was walking, a train pulled in and stopped. Doing what a good station assistant was taught to do, I completely ignored it continuing with my stroll. After a minute or so, the guard on the train waved his green flag and the train started to move. Drawing level with me, the guard glared in my direction and at my complete lack of action in directing the train and I offered a sweet smile back at him. It was just my way of saying stuff-off without the need to raise my voice, blow my whistle or wave my flag.

I had reached the platform announcement box—it was a wooden shed with glass windows and a microphone located inside. The idea was that a station assistant would look at the timetable hanging up inside and, in a voice containing a smile, announce the arrival or departure of all trains.

The actual box didn't interest me. What did was a group of four or five station assistants, all about my age, standing around doing nothing. I walked up to them, said hello and proceeded to join their group.

"Love the way you handled that train," said one of the boys.

"What train?" I asked with a smile, pretending that I hadn't even noticed one.

"The train that—" He never fully completed his sentence before another boy spoke to him,

"Oh, be quiet, dingo boy; he knows what to do!" The second boy then turned to me and explained that "dingo boy" was the nickname given to the kid as he was a bit sly but stupid, just like the Australian wild animal which sported the same name.

A second train approached and started to brake before stopping on another platform; as it did, another boy named Tom, asked me if I wanted to make an announcement.

"Why, is someone getting married?" I then added that I had no idea where the thing was coming from or going.

"Neither do we," he said laughing, "and neither does anyone else working here; fancy a cup of tea?"

Tom, I and another boy called Bob, went back down the staircase to the ground floor and across the main road to a café. We sat down and each ordered some snack food and a cup of tea which was delivered to the table at which we were sitting.

During our conversation, I told them that I was from the UK and had been here for a few months but hated both the job and Australia and couldn't wait to go back home. Tom, who was also from the UK, said that he had been in Melbourne for about four years and had immigrated with his family but still missed the 'home country'. Bob, who had a broad Aussie accent, said that he was from Newcastle and had been having rows with his family and had just packed up and run away from home, he had only been working as a station assistant for a couple of weeks.

We had all agreed that it was a crap job, but Tom promised that after our break he would show me how to make it more interesting. At that time, I was given just one word of warning, and that was to watch out for the old man who called himself the station manager. He could be a right bastard if he caught you up to no good!

As I said previously, the first time I had met the manager was in his office, and to my trained eye, he looked as though he had already passed away. I understood now why they needed fresh British blood, it was either to give the managers regular transfusions or to replace them with people who could walk a flight of stairs without a walking stick.

Bob apparently had been given numerous warnings over the short time he had worked at the station and was now on the official blacklist meaning, one more warning and all hell would be set loose for him, possibly even the sack. Not that that was anything to be concerned about, but the loss of money that went with it certainly was.

I was wondering how come if Bob came from Newcastle, he had an Aussie accent instead of a Geordie one that he should have had until it was explained to me that he was a 'fair dinkum' Aussie and was borne in Newcastle, New South Wales. A city located about one-hundred miles north of Sydney. What did 'fair dinkum' mean? Oh, it was Aussie slang meaning for real!

Finishing our tea, we walked back to the station to let the other lads go for theirs. As they left the platform, Tom explained that the way to a happy working life was to cause as much disruption as possible without getting caught. We could all ignore using the microphone to make announcements as, if passengers didn't know where they were coming from or going to, it was their fault and not ours. The microphone could, however, be used for the purpose of making funny noises or announcements that were false.

The station had platforms that were either up or down lines. The up lines led away from Flinders Street and the down lines led into it; we never ever informed passengers which one was which. Regular travellers should know which lines were which and tourists had an absolute right to enjoy their holiday—it was part of our job to add a bit of excitement to that by letting them find out for themselves if they were heading in the right direction or not.

If directly approached with a question by a member of the travelling public, we would always pretend that we couldn't speak English. Attempting some sort of Italian gobbledygook was greatly prized by the other station assistants and as there were so many Italian immigrants arriving, rail travellers would just blame the Aussie government for letting the Italians into the country in the first place.

The most important rule, however, was to never ever try and be helpful. We used to run a completion where each station assistant put a shilling a week into a hat and the lad who won the jackpot was the boy who was judged by his peers to have caused the most havoc during the week without getting caught. How we managed to get away with this, I'll never know, but it certainly brightened up what otherwise would have been a completely boring day!

One stunt that we pulled whenever possible involved the parcel switching routine. Each platform was marked with different coloured paints that were painted in small stripes to give silent signals to the employees. The most important of these marks being to show the train driver where the engine should stop. If the train stopped at the correct mark, one could follow one's line of sight and spot three other yellow marks indicating to those in the know the exact spot where the doors to the guard's van would be positioned. The yellow marks were separated into two areas of about three feet apart and were there so that parcels could be brought to the platform for either the up or down line and the guard would know that the parcels were to go in the direction of Flinders Street or on an opposite platform away from the station. The second space on each platform was the position that guards used to offload parcels destined for this station.

The station had its own parcels office at the roadside level to where the sender would drop off the parcels for urgent delivery to the station he or she had selected. Parcel office staff would deliver each parcel to the correct platform, be it up or down, and from where the station assistants would place the parcel in the correct area to be picked up by the train guard. Parcels arriving by train were to be taken down to the parcel's office whilst, parcels departing were to be placed on the correct platform and in the correct box. At least, that was the idea of the railways.

Station assistants had other ideas. For example, arriving parcels could be taken across the lines and sent back in the same direction from which they had just arrived. Departing parcels could be taken to the wrong platform to travel in the opposite direction to which they were destined to go. If this were worked professionally, a parcel merry-go-round could be achieved with parcels flying in all directions. Luckily, for us, the guard's job was to either load or unload new parcels not to check where they were actually destined for. To make it more interesting, each parcel would receive a mark each time it arrived at our station and departed again. At the end of each day, the station assistant clocking up the most marks on the same parcel would receive points; the more points, the nearer he would get to the end of the week's jackpot!

It was almost time to go home for the day, and Bob, who I had been getting along with quite well, asked me a question.

"Where do you live?" he asked.

"I rent a room about ten minutes' walk from here," I answered.

"Do you live on your own?"

"Yeah, just me," then as an afterthought, I asked, "Why do you want to know that?"

Looking rather sheepish, he told me that unless he managed to find his rent money by this evening, his landlord was going to chuck him out and that he had nowhere else to stay. My first thought was that he should not look at me for money before trying to make all sorts of excuses because it would be impossible for him to stay with me.

"It's a very small place, sort of like a bedroom with a kitchen attached."

"I won't take up much room," he countered.

"I've only got one single bed."

"I'll sleep on the floor and help you tidy up."

Feeling sorry for him, I relented and gave in. I told him that although I only had one bed, he didn't need to sleep on the floor as I had a sofa that I had forgotten to mention.

"Does that mean that you're saying yes?" He smiled.

"I guess so, but it's not permanent; as soon as you get paid, you rent a place of your own, agreed?"

"Yeah, can I move in now?"

I felt that I had no choice and nodded my head in agreement.

Chapter Fourteen

So that was how I ended up with a roommate and an Aussie one at that! We both went to the place that he was renting, a place that incidentally made the railway hostel look like a palace! We went in, and he quickly threw his belongings into two small bags and then we quietly sneaked out so his landlord wouldn't see us. Catching the train back to Footscray Station we walked the ten minutes to my place.

"This place is rather good," he said, putting his bags down and making himself at home.

"It's a lot better than that dump where you were living, I'm surprised that the landlord didn't pay you to live there instead of you paying him!"

We both giggled at the idea whilst taking off our uniform jackets and starting to relax. Bob was a very likeable person, maybe not too clever, but he had a good personality and was quite easy to get on with. We also had a few things in common; we both hated our jobs, neither had much money, we had both, in some way or the other, left home because we didn't get on with our fathers, and I think, if truth be known, we were both a bit lonely.

Whilst I went into the kitchen to prepare the daily ration of cheese on toast, he followed me in and asked if he could help. I told him that it didn't take two to make the speciality of the house, but that if he knew how to, he could light a fire in the fireplace.

By now I had started to buy an infrequent copy of the 'Melbourne Age Newspaper' so he had plenty of paper with which to use, and by the time I carried in the evening meal the fire was blazing away. Sitting on the floor with our legs crossed we chatted away mainly about what life was like for him in Newcastle and about what it was like for me in the Welsh Valleys, or Cardiff to be more precise. It was surprising just how much we had in common, and although thousands of miles apart, the things that we got up to were more or less the same.

We chatted for most of the night, and by the time the alarm clock rang to tell us it was morning and time for work, we had both only had a few hours' sleep. We quickly dressed and donned our uniforms with Bob telling me that the sofa was comfortable, and the place was much better than the place he had just left in such a hurry. Although we had only met a short while before, it felt as if we had known each other for years and certainly had no problem being in each other's company. I wonder, if I knew then what would happen later, would I have been so keen to let him stay?

Arriving at work, Bob and I joined the others in our determined efforts to bring the railway to its knees. We started the parcel merry-go-round off, made all sorts of stupid announcements and blew our whistles just to attract each other's attention. It was just like a kid's day out, but as with every other day, we soon got bored and couldn't wait for the time to arrive when we could sign out. I will never know, even to this day, how that railway managed to operate as our stupidity was being re-enacted at almost every station throughout the system.

We were about to leave at the end of our shift when the station manager, who had been skulking around, came up to me and asked if I could work an early shift the next day. Apparently, the early up line trains were lonely on their own in the morning and needed someone to blow a whistle at them. I asked him what time, and he told me '5 o'clock'.

"What, in the morning?" I gulped.

"Well, it wouldn't be in the afternoon, if it's an early shift, would it?" He smiled at his own joke, revealing his chipped teeth.

"Only for tomorrow or are you thinking of making my life even more difficult?" I growled back at him.

"Just for tomorrow will be fine, thank you," he replied in a sarcastic voice.

As we walked home, I told Bob about my shift change, and we planned the events of the next day. It was important that we worked things out properly as the guy who owned the property, where we were now both living, didn't know that there were now two of us living there. Getting to know the Aussies had proved to me that he wouldn't have cared less if there was ten of us staying in the room so long as it gave him the chance to increase the rent. So, by keeping Bob a secret from the owner prevented us from paying extra rent.

Working two different shifts presented problems that we needed to sort out. As Bob wouldn't be starting work until 7:30 and I would start at 5 o'clock, my day would finish before his. We finally concluded that we would both leave the room at the same time and he would wait in our local café known to all station assistants as the headquarters of the railway mafia. He would then go to work at the usual time. At the end of my shift, I would do the same and wait for him so that we both could go back home together. That way the landlord still would have no idea that there were two living for the price of one.

It made us laugh when I commented that, at that time of the morning, maybe they should issue us with flutes instead of whistles so that we didn't wake the train passengers up!

On arriving back at the room, we watched television for a while before, as usual, sitting on the floor with our legs crossed and complaining of just how bored we were. Eventually, Bob got a map of Australia out of his bag and showed me just where his hometown of Newcastle was located. It was about one hundred miles north of Sydney, and Sydney was about six hundred and fifty miles from our present location. I told him that I had landed in Sydney when I flew from the UK and he asked me if that was my first view of the Great Commonwealth of Australia. I told him no, that it wasn't. We had flown from Jakarta in Indonesia and then landed in a place called Darwin. Locating it on the map, I discovered that it was the capital of a state known as the Northern Territories and that it was about six hundred miles north of the central town of Alice Springs. I told Bob that I knew about 'The Alice' from a movie I once saw in a local cinema. He asked me the name, and after searching my memory for a few seconds, I remembered it was called *A Town called Alice*. Recalling some of the scenes from the movie, I felt it strange that 'The Alice' was in the same country as I was now living. It seemed like a thousand years from Melbourne.

"What's it like flying?" Bob asked suddenly.

Telling him that it was surprisingly good, I explained that I had flown here on a jet. The only type in public service since its processor and the world's first jet plane, the Comet had been taken out of service as three of them had blown themselves to pieces.

"Why did they do that?" he asked.

"Well, it wasn't as if they wanted to," I joked, "they had square windows and that weakened them when they were pressurised to fly at high altitudes," I explained, remembering what I had read in a magazine whilst sounding knowledgeable.

"Sounds dangerous to me," Bob commented.

"No, they can't be dangerous, can they? If you think about it, they wouldn't be allowed to put one hundred and fifty people on something that was going to crash, would they?"

"The Comet did!" said Bob with a giggle.

"Oh, shut up; what are you, an expert now? Look at the time; its three-thirty; I'm going to sleep."

I got into bed, and Bob made himself comfortable on the sofa. We turned the light out, then as an afterthought, I asked him, "How could we get to Alice Springs, anyway?"

"By train or hitchhiking would be the easiest," he answered as we both dozed off to sleep.

Chapter Fifteen

I woke up with a start; it was 9 o'clock in the morning making Bob late and me even later for work. We both prepared ourselves, not the least bit in a hurry, as with all the rushing in the world we would still be late so, why rush?

Arriving at the station, we nonchalantly walked up the long slope that led from the road level to the flight of stairs going up to the platforms. If we were lucky, no one would see us and perhaps, just a small 'perhaps', we had not been missed and could claim that we had been at work all along.

Our luck was out, halfway up the slope, who should we bump into? Only the Station Master himself making a grand tour of his empire. We both tried a grin accompanied by a good morning, but by the look on his miserable face, that wasn't going to work. He looked at me, and then told me to get hold of a brush and start sweeping the concourse. Glaring at Bob, he added, "And you into my office!"

Bob and I pulled faces at each other as both he and the manager disappeared into the dark depths of management.

Sweep the concourse! Like hell, that place hadn't been cleaned in years and I was not about to change history. However, I did get a brush and proceeded to lean on it watching the cars go past until I got bored with doing that and left the high-tech cleaning equipment against a wall and went up to platform level to join in with the day's games.

The other lads were hard at work, trying to disrupt the railway network as I joined in with them. We had been messing about for maybe twenty minutes when Bob slowly came up and joined us. You could tell by the look on his face that something serious had taken place in the devil's lair.

One of the lads spoke first, "You don't need to tell us, the lousy bastard sacked you?"

Bob nodded his head. "He told me that I'd already received my final warning."

"Someone should give him a final warning before pushing him under a train," I said.

"Nice idea, but he's never on the platform long enough." Tom giggled.

"So, what are you going to do now?" I asked Bob.

"Wait until you finish work, I suppose!"

"Well, you don't have to wait long; I quit, I'm sick of this job; come on, let's go!"

As we started walking back to our room, it started to rain. Just like home, I thought.

We were both sitting in our usually cross-legged position on the floor of the apartment watching television when I suddenly got up, walked across to the set, and turned it off.

"Why did you do that?" Bob asked.

"How would you like to go to the UK?" I countered with a smile.

"Are you joking? Neither of us has a passport or money!"

"Bugger passports and bugger money, I have an idea!"

I stood up and walked to my uniform jacket; putting my hand into the inside pocket, I produced the previously long-forgotten cheque book.

"You have a bank account?" a surprised-looking Bob asked.

"No, I found this book, but I used it once to buy stuff, and it works!"

"Go on," said Bob, "tell me more?"

"According to the map, Darwin is two thousand three hundred miles from here, right?"

"Yes, I guess so."

"Well, correct me if I'm wrong, but as from this afternoon, both of us are out of work, correct?"

"That was your fault; you're the one who walked out!"

"And you're the one who got the sack!" That shut Bob up.

Making most of it up on the spot, I started to explain my idea. As Darwin was the first place I landed when I came to Australia, it stood to reason that boats arriving from and going to the UK would dock there. Bob agreed. So, we first needed to get to Darwin and then stow-away on a boat. Hide until it gets to where it was going in the UK and then, when no one was looking, sneak off!

It sounded obvious to both of us that on our way to Darwin we could use trains or hitchhike and have a farewell look at Australia all at the same time.

The next day, being Friday and the end of the week, we would both be paid after which, we could come back here, collect our stuff, and disappear into the blue beyond.

What neither of us knew at that time was that ships arriving from the UK didn't go anywhere near Darwin. They arrived and departed from Sydney, Perth, Adelaide, or Melbourne and that the Melbourne departures left from a pier about ten miles away from where we were planning our great escape!

Ignorance is bliss, and for most of the night, we were awake and deep in the planning stages of our travels. We reasoned that ships bound for England would have snack bars or something similar aboard and so we should keep as much money as possible to pay for our food on the high seas. Anything needed in Australia could be paid for with a cheque. The problem of maybe getting caught using cheques that didn't belong to us was not important; as unlikely as it was to happen, it could turn into a win-win situation, saving me having to hide on a ship and hopefully getting deported.

There is possibly nothing more dangerous or disruptive than a teenager who has one thing and one thing only pressing on his mind and feels that he has nothing to lose. He will take all sorts of risks and not even consider the dangers or possible implications involved. There is simply no way he can be punished as no matter what happens in his mind, he feels that whatever he did, he did it for the right reasons!

Awake nearly all night putting together our totally unworkable plans, the following morning, we were both up and out of bed, or off the sofa, at the crack of dawn. We ate up all the bread and cheese that we had left in the place before leaving to collect our wages and, for the first time, we were the first in the queue waiting for the manager to hand the envelopes out. Handing my pay over to me, his first question was what happened to me the day before. Making sure that the money was safely in my pocket first, I informed him that as I felt Bob was treated badly, it didn't concern him what had happened yesterday to me as I resign and will no longer be working! The look that he gave me just confirmed that I had made the right decision.

Getting paid by the railway was always a pleasure especially when weighed up with the small amount of work that you had carried out to get it. Although on the other hand the small amount of cash that you received prevented most people from attempting any larger endeavours.

After my resignation, I looked straight into the eyes of the Station Manager, thinking to myself that eventually it would dawn on him that I wouldn't be coming anymore and then maybe he could sweep up the station concourse by himself!

After Bob and I returned to our room, we sat down to reconsider our first move in our master plan of going to the UK and came up with our first problem. It would be difficult, we reasoned, to hitchhike out of the city as neither of us knew which roads led in which direction or which road to take. Easier to take the train.

"Take the train to where?" I asked.

"Sydney, if you like?"

"If I like? You're the Aussie, I've no idea where to go!"

"Okay, Sydney it is then."

"How far is that from here by rail?"

"Well, not including the distance from here to Spencer Street, it must be around six hundred and fifty miles or so; we could travel overnight?"

"What do you mean not including the distance from here to Spencer Street? Some navigator you are turning out to be!"

Having decided that we wouldn't count the mileage from the room to the railway station, we laid around for most of the day studying maps of Australia until we finally left the room, carrying our bags, at about 5 o'clock in the afternoon. As I didn't know how to contact the landlord, I left the keys on the table, and just to be certain that he would find out that I had gone, I deliberately left the door ajar. I felt certain in my own mind that as soon as he noticed the door open, he would be poking his nose in and that would be if I were still living there or not!

Using our rail ID cards, we travelled by train to Spencer Street where I couldn't resist having one last look around the platforms that I had guarded so well. We ended up in the booking hall, and looking at the timetable, we quickly noted that a train with the name of the 'Southern Aurora' would depart at 8 o'clock and arrive in Sydney at around 7:30 the next morning. It was one hundred per cent first-class. Lower class passengers would have to travel on other trains.

I asked at the ticket office how much it would cost for two tickets and was told that if we wanted a twin berth cabin with a private bathroom that would cost us an arm and a leg. Would they accept a cheque? The guy nodded affirmatively, and I wrote a cheque for the full amount whilst I whispered under my breath that it would be free for us as Victorian Railways would be paying the full cost!

In an incredibly happy mood, we went to board the train. It really was first-class. The room attendant showed us around the cabin which had bunk beds and was nicely furnished; it even had table lamps. A door opened off it to reveal a nice but rather small bathroom, and the room attendant showed us how it all operated. He then stood there waiting for a tip. He didn't get one, not his lucky day really.

We had just settled in when the train moved off with a slight jerk and was soon travelling at quite a fast speed. We both had a shower, not that we needed one, but this was the only time either of us had done anything first-class, so we wanted to try it all, especially the soap and shampoo that was supplied.

After the shower, we decided it was time for dinner and so, leaving both the cabin and the shower in a complete mess, we walked the length of the corridor that linked the carriages together looking for the dining car. To get to it we had to pass through the lounge which had sofas and even a grand piano with some guy tinkering away on it; this really was luxurious living!

The food and drink were not included in the price of the ticket, but Bob and I decided to go for it anyway, and so he and I were seated at a table laid for just the two of us. Quite a large menu was offered, and although the servings were smallish, we ate many courses. Although neither of us really drank much alcohol we knocked back enough wine to make us both quite tipsy. After dinner, we decided to take coffee and brandy in the lounge car as it seemed the right thing to do. The brandy nearly choked me, but I still drank it, and Bob sat there with a silly grin and his face looking as red as a beetroot.

Laughing and drunk, we both staggered to our cabin and I fell onto the bottom bunk. Bob, after four or five attempts, managed to crawl up to his bunk, and within minutes, we were both sound asleep.

It was just after dawn when I woke up and still a little wobbly from the night before I went to the large window and looked out. Miles and miles of flat scrubland greeted me. That was all I could see. It was amazing and more like I imagined Australia to be, so different from the city, just a big open space with nothing! Suddenly, I noticed something moving from the left-hand side of the window and then I saw them! A herd of about ten or fifteen kangaroos went bounding and jumping away from the train. They were almost hopping alongside us until they bounced in a swerving motion moving away from us. It was the first time since I had landed in Australia that I felt excited. So excited I had to wake up Bob.

"Bob, hey Bob," I yelled, "There are wild kangaroos outside the train!"

He sat up with a start, "What?"

"There are wild kangaroos outside the train!"

"So, what," he mumbled, falling back down on his pillow, "there are millions in Aussie; better they're outside the train than in here!"

So much for trying to make an Australian excited!

Outline of Brian and his suitcase in the crate
© Copyright Channel 4/Reuters

Brian finally arriving at London Heathrow Airport
© Copyright Channel 4/Reuters

Freight handler tries out Brian's crate at Los Angeles Airport
© Copyright Channel 4/Reuters

Chapter Sixteen

The train was bouncing around quite a bit and I felt that it was swaying from side to side. We must have jumped the tracks and were derailing; I could feel it banging and throwing me around. It was painful to move, and I was gulping air as if I had to get my lungs full before the world ran out of the stuff.

Where was Bob? Had he been thrown out of the train carriage with all the vibration? It was pitch black, so it must still be night-time making it harder to find him. My mind began to clear, and I started to realise that I wasn't even on a train. I was still in my crate on the plane and being transported back to the United Kingdom.

I tried shaking my head to help me start to think straight, but that just met with a searing pain that shot up my neck and mixed with the headache that was so painful that it was almost impossible to open my eyes fully. And still, the drone of the plane's engines went on and on. I guessed that I must have been dreaming, or was I dreaming now?

Was it ever going to end? I was in more pain than I ever thought possible, hardly able to move, and when I did manage to rearrange part of my leg or arm, it felt as if someone was sticking a red-hot knife into my joints. Sticking a knife in and twisting it around. I must have been dying, but if dying was as painful as this, it was no wonder that we only did it once in our life. The thought of what I was thinking forced a small smile across my face.

Don't give up, fight it. Fight off the pain, I kept thinking repeatedly. I even tried singing; when I started on my journey, I had packed a book of 'Beatles' songs into the crate and although I was now unable to reach to the bottom of the box to locate it, I tried to remember some of the words to the songs—if I had been able to locate the book, it wouldn't have been much good to me anyway in the pitch darkness.

The one song that was stuck in my head and which I hummed and tried singing repeatedly was *love, love me do*. The singing didn't last too long, as the more I tried, the sorer my throat became. I was never sure if this was due to my being in the crate or my singing needed a little bit more tuning. Eventually, my throat (and ears) simply couldn't take any more of the singing, and so I shut up. I got very used to the noises from the engines, and although most of it was just a dull, loud, monstrous drone, it would change when the aircraft started to ascend or descend, and so I found myself listening intensely for the slightest change in pitch as the thought of something happening such as a landing or take-off gave me a glimmer of hope that I would arrive in London soon and in one piece.

The number one thought on my mind was how much more time would I need to spend cramped up and in agony, but at one time, even this thought was surpassed by an even more pressing one. I needed to pee, and it was becoming urgent!

I had packed a bottle for this very reason; however, my body was in such agony that to find and use it would have proved impossible. I could just sit there and pee all over myself or think of a different course of action. Peeing over myself didn't really appeal to me, but one way or another, I had to let it out. The small gaps between the slats of wood that formed the crate were my only alternatives. Somehow or the other I had to twist myself around until I was almost facing the side of the crate, and this was not going to be an easy task.

Racked with pain, I spent an eternity—or it certainly seemed like one—slowly easing myself onto my side. Hampered by both the pain and the small-sized crate I was in absolute agony. The longer that this turning process took and with the need to pee becoming even stronger left me in no doubt that the end would be catastrophic. Would I be stuck on my left hip, unable to return to a position where I could sit on my bum again, my legs completely twisted up and still peeing all over myself?

I finally managed to lodge myself in a position that was as near as I could get to actually being on my side, spent a further half an hour trying to pull down the zip on my trousers and after releasing the required appendage let rip!

Oh, the absolute relief! It was such a joy that I felt that perhaps I would keep it up until I arrived in London. However, all good things came to an end, and that was to be the same on this occasion. I had finished and all was dry well, almost all. Bearing in mind that this feat was performed in pitch darkness, it was problematic to discover if I had used the slits in the crate or not, but it seemed that around thirty per cent had flooded the bottom section of the crate and was splashing around inside it with the remaining seventy per cent waterlogging the hold of the aircraft. My main concern now was that if someone should spot the dampness in the hold, would they blame me or think that it was another crate that had chosen to take a pee.

I had just started with the reverse struggle to get back on my bum when I heard the engines change pitch. Something was happening, we were starting to descend. It was time to cross my fingers and hope that there was a runway somewhere below us. I could feel the twisting and turning of the aircraft, and it was getting easier to breathe. I surmised that we must be low and near the ground.

The aircraft seemed to make a last-minute rush quickly followed by a squeal of brakes and the engines reversing thrust, then we were belting along a runway with me being thrown in all directions. Could this be London?

Unless, since I had been absent, they had managed to change the language I soon found out that it wasn't! I could hear people boarding and blabbering on about something in a mysterious sounding language before they started moving stuff around. I sniggered at the thought of me getting out of the crate and making my way to the transit lounge to take a break. The aircraft loaders might just be in shock and ignore me; however, they'd have a bigger shock when I returned to the plane, got into the crate, closed the lid and we took off again.

It seemed to me that at this airport, a lot of freight was being moved around, and it wasn't too long before streams of light entered my humble abode. They had moved some of the boxes and crates that had originally sat on the top of my crate, so I was now in a better position to both hear and see them milling around. Two of the guys walked over and sat on top of me, well, on top of the crate, and one was kicking the side of it with the heel of his shoe. Noticing the pool of water on the floor, he stopped kicking and jumped off the crate. He disappeared for a few moments and then returned with a mop and cleared up the pee that I had so generously made for him.

More noise and the sounds of petrol-driven engines made my new-found friends move away from my crate. Accompanied by the babble of human voices and the scraping of heavy items being moved across the floor, the light in my box slowly disappeared and again became complete darkness as more freight was piled on top of me. Voices became whispers and finally tapered off to nothing leaving me, once again, in total blackness and silence.

The whine from the plane's engines returned as they started up and the heavy drone that they normally made returned to deafen me. A long run over the tarmac, and once again, we were airborne with, I hoped, the next stop being London.

86

Chapter Seventeen

The Southern Aurora express gently pulled into the Central Railway Station in Sydney as Bob and I were seated in the dining car, eating breakfast. We soon finished eating and were quickly off the train. I was lugging my suitcase along the platform, but I had soon begun to realise that I was not going to get far if I had to keep it with me. The suitcase contained all my possessions, and so I didn't want to let go of it. My idea was that as we were heading for Darwin why not send the luggage by train rather than try to carry it. Bob thought that as he only had a small backpack, he could manage it, but my suitcase, being much larger and heavier, should be sent on ahead.

Agreeing on the disposal of luggage we went to the freight section of the platform, and after paying a small fee, I was rather pleased to say goodbye to the case which, I was assured, would be waiting for us once we arrived in Darwin. Taking a breather, we sat down on a station bench, and after getting out our foldaway map, we studied it whilst contemplating our next plan of action. Giving it careful thought, we decided that we should head to a small town named Toowoomba which, although in the state of Queensland, was just about going north in the general direction of Darwin.

An overnight train would leave in the evening and it would take us around 11 hours to get there; so, after booking two tickets and having quite a few hours to wait, we decided on a tour of the central district of Sydney. Walking down one of the main roads, I turned to Bob and asked, "What do we do when we get to Toowoomba?"

"Hitchhike onto Charleville."

"How long do you think that will take us?"

"A long time, but we can camp on the way," said Bob. I was getting more and more surprised at just how big this country was, as I continued,

"If we're going to go camping, don't you think that we'll need some camping gear?"

"That's where we're going now," he said with an all-knowing smile.

'David Jones Department Store' was one of Australia's largest retail groups and possibly the Aussie version of Selfridges of Oxford Street in London. We were standing in the middle of the 'Camping and Outdoor Pursuits' department with me wondering what the hell was going to happen next. They obviously had everything we needed, but the place wasn't cheap by a long way. Nevertheless, with his usual smile, Bob said that we were going shopping, and go shopping we did.

In less than an hour we had picked a small piece of canvas and all the lightweight camping equipment you could think of; the only thing missing was something to keep us warm at night.

"Do you think we need sleeping bags or an inflatable mattress?" asked Bob.

"The bags would keep us warm, but the mattress would be more comfortable, I think."

"Okay, we'll have both," he said, adding the selected products to our list of would-be purchases.

The sales assistant took all the goods that we had selected to the cashier, and as they were ringing them up on the cash register Bob announced that he wanted them to be charged to an account. What the hell was he talking about? I was gobsmacked and thought he had taken leave of his senses. Nevertheless, the cashier gave him the receipt and told him that he should take it to the fourth floor for credit approval.

We both sat on a sofa, waiting for him to meet with the credit people when I quietly asked him what was going on.

"My mother has a credit account here, and as she's done nothing for me, I'm doing nothing for her," he replied, "I'm charging it to her account!" He then went on as to how they had never helped him, caused him many problems, and so it was payback time!

"You're mad," I said, but before I had any chance to add anything else, they had called him into the credit office.

Five minutes later, we were both laughing and walking out of the store with his purchases. I still, to this day don't know what had been said in the credit office, but they had authorised the sale!

We slowly walked back to the railway station and after buying something to eat we sat around waiting for the train that would take us to Toowoomba to arrive at the platform. Whilst we waited, we split the camping gear into two backpacks, one for Bob and one for me, making sure that each pack weighed about the same.

The train finally pulled into the station and we walked along its length until we arrived at the carriage in which our tickets allowed us to travel. Well, what can I say? We were certainly going into the Australian outback; the carriage seats were more like park benches than train seats. Made of wood, the actual seating was nailed in strips onto the frame, there was no upholstery just the strips of wood forming both the seat and the backrest. What a change from our first-class arrival into Sydney!

We had only been seated about ten minutes when our bums and backs began to ache, but before we had time to change our tickets to a better class of carriage, the train had started to move taking us on our twelve-hour journey through hell.

And hell, it was! Trying to get some sleep proved almost impossible. With our aching backs and bums, the train zigzagged for mile after mile at what seemed to me to be the slowest speed the driver could make the thing move without stopping.

Hour after miserable hour both the time and the train dragged on with Bob and me having to stand up at regular intervals and walk around as much as space would permit to relieve the aches and pains caused by the wooden seating. No matter how many times and for how long we stood we still eventually had to sit back down again. Then, within ten minutes of sitting back down, the cycle would start all over again, and so it continued throughout the entire night.

Finally, I dozed off to sleep only to wake up again perhaps twenty minutes later, just in time to watch the dawn breaking. The sun soon started to rise showing us the unending miles of flat Australian outback that was home to the Australian sheep industry.

Amazingly, Bob seemed to be asleep or at least pretending to be—he liked people to think that he was an Aussie man and could put up with all sorts of discomfort.

There was a change in the shaking and cliquey-clacking sound of the train wheels. We were slowing down, maybe the driver wanted us to get off and push the thing I thought. But no, some buildings came into view and we gradually came to a complete halt at what seemed to be some excuse for a railway station.

The train inspector came around, telling the few passengers that had managed to survive the night that we would be here for about an hour or so, and Bob and I with some elation, stood up and left the compartment.

We stepped down off the so-called train onto a long wooden platform that seemed much too long and spotted a few dogeared and old wooden buildings dotted along its length. Walking toward the buildings we came across the guy who was the inspector on the train and discovered that yes, we could get a cup of tea and that we would remain at this station until the down train to Sydney came through leaving the up line open for us. It was only then that I realised that we were travelling on a single-track system, and until that train arrived, we were going nowhere!

Going up to the building that served as the station café we ordered two teas and would have ordered something to eat except for the fact that they had nothing. As there were only about ten people travelling in the entire group of carriages and one train each day, I suppose that was just about understandable.

This was my first look at the great Australian outback and quite apart from it seeming to go on forever, everything appeared to be covered with dust. Reddish dust, to be more precise, and it was everywhere. The heat was the other thing that was noticeable, and even at this time of the morning the thermometer was beginning to rise. Bob and I found a patch of shade and sat down on the wooden platform to await the arrival of the other train.

Whilst we were waiting, I mentioned to Bob that I had heard a story of this place one time. "What story?" he asked.

"It was about two Aussie men talking in a bar. One says, 'A girl I met in Sydney gave me a sexually-transmitted disease'."

His mate replied, "You were lucky, in this place you would have had to pay for it!"

"That supposed to be funny?"

"I think so," I replied, doubling over with laughter.

No one seemed to care much about time—or anything else for that matter, they were all lying around doing nothing, just thinking of the sheep they had loved! I mentioned this to Bob and managed to get a slight smirk.

The hour passed by without any sign of life or anyone apart from me noticing the time go by. The first hour was followed by a second one before I noticed any sign of life from our fellow passengers. There was a distinct movement from the others, and I heard the noise too. It was the sound of another train approaching. Quietly at first, the noise built up and the second train came into view. With a whoosh of pneumatic brakes, it came to a halt. A shout went up "all aboard", and we were finally ready to depart for Toowoomba.

Chapter Eighteen

It took another three hours of train travel before we arrived in Toowoomba, but finally, we were there and could leave the train for good. The place could be best described as a small to medium-sized town with the most memorable thing about it being the road that led out of the place. Bob and I were, however, hungry and decided that we would find somewhere to eat before starting to hitchhike to our next destination.

From the station to the main street was only a hundred yards or so, and that was lined on either side by a row of small shops with a pub placed somewhere in between them. Both rows of shops were fronted by a wooden canopy that ran the full length of the street to protect would-be shoppers from the direct rays of the sun, and which warmed the whole place up like an oven. The only café in the street was open; so, after going inside and seating ourselves at a table, we ordered breakfast.

"Where do we go from here?" I asked Bob between mouthfuls of food. He took our map out of his backpack, carefully unfolded it and studied it for a minute or two before telling me in his best explorer-sounding voice that Charleville would be our best bet.

"How far is that?"

"About three hundred and sixty miles," he replied with this new know-all voice, "in the opposite direction of Brisbane."

"Are we already in Queensland?"

"Yeah, and now we have to start to go inland and away from the coast." He carefully folded our map and placed it in the backpack. As he was putting it away, he looked at me before adding, "And I think we should buy a gun each!"

"A gun each, have you flipped your lid?" I asked in shock more than surprise. To be told back in the UK that we should buy guns was completely unheard of and, up until that time, I had never even seen a real gun in close-up.

"Won't we get stopped by the police if we carry guns?" I asked him.

"Nope, they're legal here, you know. At least, rifles are!"

"Why do we need rifles anyway?" I replied, scarcely believing my ears.

"You never know who or what you'll meet in the outback; better to be prepared."

"Prepared for what?"

"For anything; there's a gun shop a few doors down the street; I seen it on our way here!"

"A gun shop; this place is getting more like the Wild West by the minute."

We left the café and walked the few yards down to where the town's gun shop was located. On entering, I was amazed to see that three walls of the place were covered by cabinets, some with glass doors, some without, but all full of every type of gun that you could possibly think of. Pistols, rifles, shotguns and some of which I had no idea what they were called filled every available space. With a smile, Bob spoke to the sales assistant.

"Hi, we're looking to buy some rifles," he said.

"Well, you've come to the right place; what sort of thing are you looking for?"

"We need advice on that; something that we don't need a licence for," answered Bob.

"That narrows it down a bit," the guy replied. "What are you planning to use them for?"

"Hunting," Bob quickly replied.

".22 automatics should suit you," said the guy, turning around and taking one down from a cabinet before passing it over for inspection. "It can hold fifteen bullets in a single cartridge."

Bob grabbed the rifle and started to examine it in detail. "How much is it?" he asked.

The assistant got hold of a price list, and after looking up the price of the gun he told us how much he wanted.

"Does that include telescopic sights?" Asked Bob.

"Why, are you blind?" I shot at him, but before he could answer me, the shop assistant butted in.

"No, they come as extra if you want them?" The guy then reached under the counter and, after producing a cardboard box, opened it and took out a set of rifle sights before taking the rifle back from Bob and clipping them onto the gun.

"What do you think?" Bob asked me, "shall we buy two?"

For the first time since we entered the shop, I spoke seriously, "We don't need two; one will do, plus a few boxes of bullets!"

"Are you sure?" Bob asked, looking slightly disappointed.

"At that price, I'm absolutely sure; will you take a cheque for one?"

The assistant nodded his head, confirming that it would be no problem, and that if we bought the sights, we could have a free rifle case to carry it all in. Sounded like a good deal for a worthless piece of paper, so I wrote a cheque for the amount asked for and Bob and I left the shop carrying our new weapon of war. As soon as we were out of the shop, Bob couldn't wait to speak to me,

"Why didn't we buy two, they would both have been free?"

"If we didn't get any, it would still have cost the same, idiot!"

"What?"

"Do you know how much two would have cost? If we had said two, he might have said no to a cheque, then we'd have ended up with none, idiot!" I answered.

"I never thought of that!"

"I didn't expect you to think, do you know why Jesus wasn't born in Australia?"

"What? No, why?"

"Jesus wasn't born here because no one could find three wise men and a virgin!"

"I suppose you think that's funny," said a grinning Bob.

"Pretty much so." I grinned back. "Why don't we do a deal?"

"What deal?"

"You keep thinking of how to get us to Darwin." I laughed. "And I'll think of all the rest worth thinking about!"

We walked further along the main street toward the edge of town when I suddenly stopped dead. "What now?" asked a quite mystified Bob who had no idea why I had stopped.

"I've got a new idea! Follow me."

With Bob following I crossed the road and went into a photographic shop. Once inside, I inquired as to what eight-millimetre cine cameras they had in stock. They only had one, a wind-up, single-lens job. "That will do," I told the assistant after examining it. In addition, I ordered three rolls of eight-millimetre film and paid for the whole lot with a cheque.

"What's that for?" Bob asked after we were back outside on the main street.

"You shoot the world, and I'll film it for prosperity, you got your gun, I got my camera."

We were becoming dab hands with worthless cheques—the world seemed to be too good to be true.

Holding on to our new possessions and our backpacks, we carried on walking until we reached the edge of town. It didn't take too long before we were both tired out from all the walking and the heat, so we flopped out on the side of the road. With Bob examining his new rifle in detail and me doing the same with the camera. We both happily passed away an hour or so before putting them away. Picking up our backpacks we started to walk along the tarred road in the general direction of Charleville. The sun was beating down, and it wasn't long before we sat down a second time feeling exhausted. We both realised by now that for all our carefully-made plans, we had forgotten something. With the glare and the heat from the sun our heads felt as though they were splitting open, we had forgotten the Aussie-style hats to protect ourselves.

As we were pondering just what to do to correct this oversight, a dust cloud in the distance forewarned us that a vehicle was approaching. Immediately forgetting our aching heads, we took up a hitchhiking position and awaited the approach of the on-coming vehicle.

The dust got to us first, followed very quickly by a large ten-wheeled truck. The braking of the vehicle caused an even larger dust cloud, nevertheless we ran through it and up to the driver's cab.

"Where you off to fellas?" The driver shouted down to us.

"Charleville," we shouted back, peering through the cloud of dust and trying to see him.

"Come on, get in, I can take you fifty miles or so."

We clambered into the cab and were soon settling down to our first hitchhiking ride. The driver explained that he could take us a short way, but that he was eventually going to be turning off the road and heading in another direction. He would drop us at that junction before turning off. Chatting and passing the time we explained to him that we were really going to Darwin and that we intended to hitch most of the way.

"Darwin," he laughed and said, "That's bloody thousands of miles away."

"No problem, we've got a lot of time," I replied.

"You'll need it," he joked, "why are you going there?"

"We're really going to England, but we need to get a boat when we reach Darwin."

Looking at us as though we were daft, the subject was changed to the rifle.

"Nice piece of equipment, can you use it?" he asked.

"Of course, we can," answered Bob rather unconvincingly.

The driver laughed even more, and we continued in silence for a while until he decided that it was time to stop for a short break and to relieve himself.

We were all hanging around outside the truck, smoking a cigarette when the driver suddenly asked if he could look at the rifle. "sure," said Bob, "it's a pretty good one, right?". He spoke in a voice that sounded more like he was begging for someone to confirm that he had made the right purchase.

"It sure looks pretty good."

Bob jumped up into the cab and jumped back down again with the rifle. He handed it to the driver.

"I used to be a pretty good shot a few years back, you mind if I try my luck."

"What on?" Bob asked.

"If you look to the right a bit carefully, you might spot that emu about two hundred yards into the bush?"

"Yes, I see it," we both answered at the same time.

The driver raised the rifle to his shoulder and looked down the barrel.

"He won't hit that," Bob whispered to me, "it's much too far away!"

The driver played with the rifle for a minute or so before he looked through the scope and took aim. With the loudest bang that I have ever heard the gun exploded and a wisp of smoke came from the barrel. The emu dropped to the ground as if it were hit by lightning and the driver lowered the rifle.

"Your scope needs adjusting," he said.

"Why?" asked Bob in astonishment. "You hit it!"

"Come on, I'll show you." All three of us then ran to where the dead emu was lying.

"Look at it," the driver said, pointing at the bird, "I aimed for its head, but the bullet hit its body, the crosshairs in the scope need raising a little."

"Still a surprisingly good shot," I said.

"Not bad," commented Bob.

"Could have been better," said the driver.

We all got back into the lorry and we drove in almost silence for perhaps half an hour before the driver pulled to the edge of the dirt road and stopped.

"Well, this is where we part company, lads," he said, "I have to go right, and for Charleville, you'll need to go straight on!"

Gathering all our stuff together, we thanked him for his help and jumped down from the lorry. With a large dust storm, the lorry pulled away and after turning right it slowly disappeared.

"It was a fluke," said Bob as soon as the lorry had gone.

"What was?"

"That shot with the emu."

"Well, he hit it, didn't he?"

"That's why I'm telling you it was a fluke; even I couldn't have hit that!"

We started walking along the dirt road, but Bob was still rambling on about the driver's shot. It was obvious that like the emu his feathers had been ruffled. He suddenly stopped walking and I came to a halt alongside him.

"What now?" I asked.

"Shush," he whispered pointing off to the right, "there's a rabbit!"

Sure enough, about fifty feet away from where we were standing, a rabbit was merrily jumping up and down enjoying itself. We slowly took off our backpacks and placed them on the ground. Bob raised the rifle and took careful aim. A second bang of the day filled the air.

"I got it," yelled Bob, "come on!" We began running in the direction of the rabbit. Arriving at the spot where the rabbit should have been, we looked around and found—nothing!

Searching the scrub for five minutes gave the same result.

"So, where is it?" I asked.

"It's here, keep looking!" We both continued to look, but all we found was a small hole in the ground. "Must be its burrow," said Bob.

"Never mind its burrow, where's the bloody rabbit you shot?" Bob carefully thought for a few moments before explaining his theory.

"It must have been standing outside its burrow and when I shot it, it was so surprised it fell back into the hole!"

"I've got a better suggestion."

"What?"

"You missed." I laughed.

Bob, however, would have none of it and for the next few hours we argued as to whether he had hit the rabbit or, by a stroke of luck, managed to hit the ground somewhere near to where the rabbit was playing.

Chapter Nineteen

The sun was beginning to dip beneath the horizon and settle as night began to creep across the flat land where we had decided to stop for the night. It was to be our first night of camping beneath the stars, and so, we needed to practice and work out exactly how to make a camp.

Opening our backpacks, we began unpacking the contents and after laying it all out on the ground we quickly began to survey our position. The first thing that was needed was a few tree branches to use as tent poles. These we soon chopped down from around the campsite and then formed into an igloo-type shape. Then we unfolded the waterproof sheet that we had purchased in Sydney and threw it over the branches.

That job completed; we blew up the inflatable mattresses and carefully placing them inside our new tent covered them with the sleeping bags. Home-from-home, it really looked comfortable and we both stood for a while just admiring our handiwork.

After collecting a few twigs and small branches we lit a campfire and sat around it both feeling rather pleased with our efforts. We stayed around the fire for ten minutes or so as the day turned into the pitch darkness of night-time. The flickering of the fire was the only light as being in the bush, miles from the nearest town or hamlet, meant that there was no glow from the lights that one would expect to show from the local electrical source of a town or city.

We chatted for a while before the thought hit us that we were feeling rather hungry, but during our careful planning, we had forgotten to buy any food. Never mind, it was only one night, and after all, we had the rifle so tomorrow we could go hunting and live off the land. With stomachs rumbling, we placed all our camping equipment inside the tent and crawled in, looking forward to a good night's sleep.

It certainly was comfortable with the inflatable mattresses taking all the hardness off the ground and within minutes we were both sound asleep.

The sound of the thunder and a flash of lightning woke us both up with a start. It was raining so heavily it was difficult to hear each other talking and the rain was really lashing down against the waterproof sheet. With each flash of lightning the inside of the tent turned from complete blackness into almost broad daylight whilst in the broad expanse of open space the thunder was echoing, making it sound twice as loud as it should have been. It would have been scary if we weren't both men of the outback. At least that is what we were trying to convince ourselves.

The waterproof sheet that was covering us was being whipped up and down by the wind and the weight of the falling rain. The power that was being unleashed in that storm was unbelievable but, if nothing else, we were still dry whilst the sheet held out against the elements.

Sitting there in our sleeping bags, fully awake and with our knees bent into our chests we waited with fingers crossed for the storm to abate. Suddenly, and before we had time to react, a big gust of wind blew our waterproof sheet, clean off the wooden frame that we had erected, and it disappeared into the blackness. It left us feeling like we were sitting in a shower with the rain taking the place of the showerhead and pouring down on top of us.

The storm continued for a while, and we were unable to do much other than sit there and get wet. There was nowhere to seek shelter, and apart from the flashes of lightning, we were surrounded by the complete darkness and were unable to see a hand in front of our faces. The rain finally started to ease up and eventually stopped, leaving us completely soaked and sitting in sleeping bags half full of water.

We spent the rest of the night in very soggy conditions, hungry, cold and unable to sleep. When the dawn broke, we could fully see the extent of the damage to our camp. Everything was waterlogged, but luckily, our waterproof sheet was still with us, just tangled up in a tree a few yards away.

Feeling sorry for ourselves, we took all our camping gear and spread it out in the sunlight to dry it. That also included the clothes we had been wearing and those that had been left in the backpacks. We were left in a totally ruined camp, standing around in just our still-wet underwear and feeling very cold indeed.

It didn't take long before everything started to dry out and the sun started to warm us up. A further hour and we could put our clothes back on and start folding everything else up to put it all back in the backpacks.

We learnt a big lesson that night, if you make a camp and use tree branches and a waterproof sheet as a tent, don't forget to tie the sheet onto the branches then, in the case of a storm, everything will hold together and protect you from the weather!

Within a short time, everything had returned to normal and even the ground had virtually dried out. We decided that as the camp had brought us no luck, we would forget it and continue with our travels. When moving, we had already made a decision that we would stick to the roadside as we—or at least Bob—had heard that people who had wandered away tended to get lost and that some had never been seen again.

With our backpacks attached, we started walking along the side of the road. The further we walked the hotter we became and the more we were sweating. The local flies seemed to realise this and started to follow us everywhere. Hundreds of them, all buzzing around you. It didn't matter how often you waved your hand or even shouted at them; they were soon back to annoy you again.

We had walked perhaps four or five miles accompanied by the flies when, a few hundred yards off the road we spotted a billabong. For those readers who have not had the pleasure and joy of being stuck in the Australian outback, a billabong is a large hole in the ground filled with water. In civilised countries, a pretty one might be called a lagoon or pond!

The Australian version was built for the sole purpose of allowing the local sheep or cows somewhere to get a drink of water. Seeing a billabong might lull you into believing that a farm or, in the local lingo, a 'station' might be nearby. Don't be fooled. It could be a false sense of security as some of these stations could be ten, fifteen or even fifty square miles in size and would take the station workers or owners two or three days to travel around on horseback with them sleeping outdoors at night!

The 'station house' being near or far didn't bother us as we, accompanied by the flies, made a beeline for the water. They made these billabongs deep, and after the rain last night this one was full. With the heat and the sweat we had produced it looked inviting and so, stripping off our clothes, we were soon splashing around in the murky water. It served us as both a swimming pool and a bath and we took full advantage of both. With the amount of soap, we were using any sheep that drank from the water after we had finished would be blowing bubbles for a week. Between our splashing around, we even took time to shout insults at the flies who, for some unknown reason, had decided not to join us in the water.

After some time playing around and even trying to drown each other Bob and I ended up crawling out and sitting on the bank. I was just going to lie on my back and soak up the sun when Bob yelled an urgent sounding "Keep still" at me. Expecting at the very least to be attacked by a kangaroo or rabid sheep, I froze.

"What's up?" I almost whispered.

"Keep still." He paused.

"Where's the cigarette lighter?"

"Are you completely mad?" I asked, still whispering, and holding myself stock still. "You want me to keep still while you smoke a cigarette?"

"Shut up and keep still!"

With me still not moving he went to my trouser pocket and took out the lighter. Returning, he uttered a further "Keep still!" and then after flicking the lighter he really did light up a cigarette. He blew on it until the end was red hot then moved it toward me.

My first thought was that hunger had got to him, set his brain wonky and he was about to cook me but no, he brought the cigarette closer to my arm, held it there for a few moments, and a big black thing fell off!

"What the hell is that?" I asked in horror whilst still not daring to move.

"It's a bloodsucker," he replied whilst removing a further two of them from my back. "They bite into you and suck your blood!"

After he had checked me out, I examined him and found just one attached to his back which, after taking a few drags of the cigarette I burnt off. I then closely examined the offending creatures before saying, "They're leeches, big black leeches!"

"Yeah, that's them," he said before adding, "they can be dangerous if left on, they carry toxins!"

"So, do you, with you being an Australian!" He just pulled one of his wacky smiles.

I had suggested that we make a new camp to spend the night alongside the billabong, but that idea had been rejected by Bob the mountain man as with us not knowing where the farmhouse was located, the farmer might just come to inspect his water supply. After finding us, he might just turn us off his land. With the sun beating down and the flies starting to return to us again, we branched off the dirt road and headed across the paddocks of land having really no idea where we were going except, according to Bob, in the right direction as he was navigating by the sun. The fact that he would have problems finding a corner shop in a big city had some bearing on his powers of navigation.

After plodding on for perhaps a further couple of miles we came across a series of anthills. Made from earth, they had been baked in the sun for so long they were solid. From the ground they reached five or six feet into the air and were quite large in diameter. I was informed that each hill was home to millions of fire ants that would attack and kill anything that managed to get in their way. We managed to fire a few rounds from the rifle into one of them to prove how solid it was. Each bullet took a chunk out of the mound, but we didn't see any ants. They must have been having a nap whilst trying to avoid the afternoon sun.

Avoiding the sun was something that we were not phenomenally successful at doing, and after only a short distance of travelling, we would become exhausted, leaving us no option other than to stop and rest for a while. By my calculations, it would take forever to get to Darwin and start our long sea voyage to England. However, we had started this mammoth adventure, and there was no way to turn back now. Even if we had decided that we had nowhere else to go, so in the footsteps of some of the world's greatest explorers we had to continue even if the whole project was consistent with the blind leading the blind.

We pressed on walking, and after a while, we arrived at a riverbank. The river was quite unexpected however very welcomed as it offered us drinking water. The water wasn't very deep but surprisingly for Australia, it seemed to be clean. We drank the water and then cupping our hands together, we splashed it over our heads and faces to cool us down. We were so pleased with our find that we instantly decided that this was where we'd make our next camp.

Using tree branches, we again assembled a frame which we covered with our waterproof sheet—this time not forgetting to tie it down. We gathered twigs and made a fire, before making everything else camp shape. Only one thing was missing—food! If only there was a '7/11' nearby things would have been perfect.

As the nearest shop to us could be anywhere up to one hundred miles away, we gave up on the idea of going shopping and later decided to go on a hunting trip instead. Getting the rifle and a pocket full of bullets together we set out. As we had no wish to get lost, we stayed pretty close to the riverbank so if the worst came to the worst and we got lost, forgetting Bob's directions from the sun, we could make our way back to camp following the river. We had only gone thirty yards when we discovered the rotting body of a sheep in the river. It was bobbing up and down in the clean water that we had been drinking. From then on, we boiled all the water and allowed it to cool down before we drank it.

Being the expert campers, hitchhikers, and hunters that we thought we were, we wandered through the scrub laughing, giggling and singing the latest pop songs that came into mind, but we didn't manage to comprehend how come we had yet to see any animal worth eating. In fact, seeing any animals at all, worth eating or not!

Many of the tree branches were full of a type of Australian parrot known locally as kookaburras, and even they seemed to be laughing at us. After a while we came across a kangaroo that stood quite still and was just staring us out. To this day, I put the reason for it not moving down to one of two things; either it was too old to hop and was waiting for a bus or it was already dead! Neither of these ideas perturbed Bob who, with a lightning flash of speed, whipped the rifle off his shoulder and pointed it in the rough direction of the animal. He took aim and gently squeezed the trigger. The gun jerked as a bullet quickly sped out of the barrel contacting a kookaburra that toppled over and fell out of a tree.

Still not dismayed, Bob changed direction with his pointing of the rifle and let off a barrage of five or six shots, in the belief that the more he threw at the kangaroo, the more chance something would hit it. With the sound of the bullets echoing around the paddock the kangaroo finally took the hint and, with a look akin to disgust, slowly hopped away.

"What happened?" I asked him.

"He was too quick for me," replied Bob without the slightest smile on his face.

"Can you eat kookaburras?" I asked with a grin, to which I got a gruff "No" as the reply.

That night, we had a sleepless time. Dozing on and off, we would wake each other up with the sound of our stomachs growling at the slight thought of food. Something had to be done before the newspapers reported a story of the two fearless hunters who starved to death in the Aussie outback.

Chapter Twenty

We both woke up before dawn with the thought of food playing on our minds and stomachs. The length of time seemed much longer than the two days since we had last eaten, and we were determined to do something about it.

The only way we could possibly eat was to catch something that we could cook on an open campfire and I must admit that the idea didn't really appeal to me. However, hunger is what hunger does and we really had no choice.

Bob, with his years of shooting practice was eager to get going, and so, leaving the camp behind we once again set out on safari. Neither of us had any idea where we were going or, for that matter, what we were going to catch, but with hunger pains rumbling in our stomachs we just had to find something.

Following the same track that we had followed the previous day, we walked for maybe an hour, sitting down at regular intervals to take a rest from the sun and to also allow Bob to play with the gun and think that he was Ned Kelly.

Unlike the first time, we were quiet, no singing, giggling, or laughing; hunger was the number one priority and gave us added urgency. Out of the blue, we suddenly spotted something moving in the distance and both of us dropped to our knees so that the scrub would give us some sort of cover. Bearing in mind Bob's expertise in shooting, we needed to get as close to whatever it was to even be in with a chance of shooting it. I should point out that although I had tried shooting the rifle a few times, my shots were about on par with Bob's, and so, I gave him the right to be the hunter, if for no other reason than it gave me the opportunity to show off my prowess at sarcasm whenever he made a cock-up.

There was also another reason in letting him keep the rifle, the thought of killing something didn't appeal to me. I was more the animal lover type of person. I kept both of my reasons to myself and as most of the sarcasm fell on deaf ears, I reasoned that there was no reason in telling him.

Half crawling, we moved forward with our eyes focused on the spot where we had spotted 'the thing' move. We slowly crept up to the possible target and were both quite surprised to find that it wasn't one but more like one hundred and one or more targets and all edible. We had chanced upon a flock of sheep, roast lamb on legs! There were just two obstacles to contend with, the first being who was going to shoot one, and the second being who was going to carve it up!

I had already decided that I would leave both of those delights to Bob whilst I appointed myself as head chef and would do the cooking. The nearest I had managed before today to get to meat, was to eat it and so I foresaw some challenges just on the cooking side. Never mind the slaughter and butchering of poor old *Larry the Lamb*.

By now, we were about fifty yards from our proposed meal with both of us lying flat on our stomachs. I didn't dare look at any of the targets on an eye-to-eye basis as eye contact would have put me off-eating meat for life. At the same time, I was hoping that Bob was not so worried and was using his eyes, as the thought of another kookaburra giving up the ghost to satisfy our hunger didn't appeal to me either.

"Are you ready?" Bob whispered to me.

I should have replied, "About as ready as I'll ever be," but I took the easy way out and just whispered, "Yeah!"

I had no idea why he was asking me if I were ready, as it was, he who would be doing all the shooting.

Bang, bang, bang—about six shots rang out; he had no intention of missing this time.

The noise and I guess, the flying objects racing toward them startled the sheep which all made a run to get away from us. All, being the word! Using the word in English as a determiner, they had all gone, there were none left! I opened my eyes, which had been closed at the time of the shooting, just in time to watch them all running away, that was—except one!

About fifty yards away from where they had been standing, Larry had stopped running, he walked unsteadily for a few feet and then collapsed in a big ball of wool on the ground.

Bob was ecstatic; he had finally hit something that wasn't a kookaburra!

With both of us yelling at the top of our voices, we ran toward dinner. In my mind's eye I could see it surrounded by roast potatoes and two vegetables. When we arrived at the gravesite, I gave Bob the large knife that I had been carrying on the belt of my trousers and nodded, as if to say, "Okay, now cut it up!"

With me looking away slightly, he dutifully obeyed with his only question being,

"What parts do we want?"

"The edible ones," I offered in return.

Bob should have studied to be a surgeon or, at the very least, a butcher as within ten minutes he had skilfully removed all the main parts and we were heading back to our campsite carrying between us more lamb than a butcher's shop would have sold in a week.

Arriving back, and without wasting any time, we lit a roaring fire and laid the meat out next to it. After having a debate on the subject, we decided that we should cook it all as it would last longer if cooked than leaving it raw. Apart from the lasting effect cooking would have on it, it also looked a lot better after the flames had got on with its job. We started cooking the lamb until it resembled something that could be bought at a delicatessen and then we both ate our fill. It was delicious and tasted fresh.

What to do with the large amount that was left over? If we left it on the ground, it could be stolen by wild animals and even if no wild animal fancied it, there were always the ants; they would eat anything! This was one of those times we wished we'd bought a refrigerator with us, although carrying one of those things on our backs – and especially one made by 'General Motors' – wouldn't have been easy and wouldn't have given us the hoped-for 'bushranger' appearance.

Going deep into thought for a few minutes, we easily solved the problem! We would tie it all to the branches of a tree where it would stay cool and fresh and be safe until our next meal. Climbing the selected tree, we picked low branches, tied it all up and jumped back to the ground. The sun had gone down hours before, and with all that excitement plus a full stomach, all we could think of was sleeping. We crawled into our tent and within minutes were both fast asleep.

It was quite late the next morning when we woke up. We checked that our supply of roast lamb hadn't been disturbed by anything before lighting a fire and reheating up a leg. We had large portions on our plates and were complimenting ourselves on just how delicious it was when a sudden noise attracted my attention.

It was the horse I saw first. I elbowed Bob to shut up and listen before pointing in the direction where the movement had caught my attention. The horse and rider then came into full view, barely five yards away from us. With our mouths wide open and agape, we stared at the guy.

"Good day, fellas," the rider said to us. Standing up, we both wished him a totally hollow sounding "good day".

"You fellas out camping?" he drawled.

"Yeah, we're making our way to Darwin," I answered.

"You've got a long way to go!" Bob and I just nodded our heads like a pair of muppets.

The guy, who was dressed a bit like Ned Kelly without the metal helmet the outlaw was famous for wearing, slung one leg over the horse so that he was sitting side-saddle; he fiddled around in his shirt pocket and, producing a pouch of rolling tobacco and a pack of Rizla papers, he proceeded to roll himself a cigarette. He lit it up without saying a word whilst Bob and I, both noticed that he kept glancing at our store of roast lamb that was still hanging from a tree only a few yards from where he was sitting on his horse. He took a long drag from his cigarette before he spoke.

"Say, you lads haven't seen a flock of sheep on your travels, have you?"

Bob and I, both answered at the same time.

"No," said Bob.

"Yes," said I, "they were over there." As I spoke, I pointed in the opposite direction to which we had seen the sheep. The guy kept glancing at our larder tree and the conversation came to a halt. He waited thirty seconds before he asked,

"Are you sure?"

"No, not really," I answered before trying a grin to see if that would help the situation. The guy still sounded friendly, so I continued.

"Are you the station owner?"

"No, I'm a station hand, and I've got to find that flock before I can go on a seven-day holiday!" He was still glancing at the lamb.

"What would the owner say if he found out someone had shot one of his sheep?" I asked.

"Have to find out first, wouldn't he?"

"You mean that you wouldn't tell him?"

"I've got no real reason to do that this very minute, especially if someone helped me out!"

Bob and I relaxed a bit.

"They're over there," we both said at the same time, pointing in the right direction and grinning at him. He grinned back which, I felt, was a good sign.

"They're only about fifteen minutes away!" I added for good measure.

"Why'd you shoot one," he asked, still smiling.

"Because we had no food and were bloody hungry," answered Bob.

"That sounds like a fair dinkum excuse."

"That means you're not going to say anything, right?" I ventured.

"A deal's a deal mate, you told me where to find the flock, and in return, I'll keep my word!"

"Jesus, thanks, mate," said Bob, grinning, as if the three of us had been friends for a lifetime.

"How long are you planning to camp here?"

"Few days maybe," I answered.

"Well, if you need some tucker, just come over to the station house; it's a mile or so over there," he said, pointing with his hand, "I'll see you right!"

We both thanked him for his help, and he trotted off in the general direction of the flock of sheep.

"You think that we should visit the station house?" I asked Bob after the station hand had left us.

"Are you bloody joking, we're getting out of here right now, in case he changes his mind!"

Chapter Twenty-One

Packing our stuff away quickly and not forgetting our lamb, we made a beeline for the dirt road with the intention of thumbing a lift. After waiting a few hours without even the sight of a vehicle but with the idea that at any moment, a group of mad horsemen might descend on us and, at best charge us with cattle rustling or some such thing, we started to walk.

We really weren't prepared for this type of travel at all, and within minutes, our former friends (the herd of flies) joined us again. We had no idea how they knew where we were going but they always managed to find us. Constantly trying to flick them away with our hands, the flies thought that we were playing games with them, the more we flicked the more they tried and succeeded in annoying us.

Sitting down at the side of the road, we just gave up. With the sun beating down and the flies still buzzing around us, we just couldn't take it anymore. This strip of dirt was the main road to Charleville, but it seemed to handle only three or four vehicles a day, hardly a traffic jam! About then, we had a sudden flash of inspiration. Why not sleep during the day and travel at night? No sun and even the flies would be sleeping! Putting this brainwave into immediate effect, we laid back and dozed off.

We woke up just as the sun was starting to set. The weather was much cooler and our friends, the flies, had all disappeared except for one who we managed to catch and squash. Perfect walking conditions, but we needed to implement our rule, only walk on the edge of the road and under no circumstances veer away from it even if we thought we could spot a short-cut. Many people had, in the past walked away from the road and within minutes managed to get themselves completely lost, many had even died. In a land where everything looked the same losing one's way was an easy and dangerous thing to do.

With all the holes in the ground, walking during the night was not the easiest thing to do however, we plodded further and further on frequently looking behind us in the hope of seeing some form of transport. During one of these turns, I spotted a light maybe three or four miles behind us and obviously on the road. Finally, we had the possibility of getting a lift. We stopped walking and waited, and waited, and waited, but the vehicle didn't appear to be getting any closer. After a while, Bob asked me if I had noticed anything unusual.

"Such as what?" I asked him.

"Such as any noise?"

We both struggled as hard as we could, trying to hear the noise of an approaching vehicle but, try as we may there was dead silence. Both of us knew that in the outback and especially at night the slightest noise would travel for miles and no driver would turn off his engine, even if he had stopped for a while for fear of the engine not starting again and yet, we could see the light from a vehicle but couldn't hear it?

We slowly started to walk again constantly looking at the light behind us when Bob started to tell me about an Australian ghost story that apparently was pretty well known in these parts (how he knew that I'll never know as he came from hundreds of miles away). The ghost looked like a car headlight and, from a safe distance away, followed lonely travellers never giving up until it had driven them mad! The story was accompanied by a few Woo's and other weird sounds put in for good measure and affect by the storyteller.

"Well, it won't change us as we must be mad for being here in the first place!"

"This is serious; I'm not joking, you know?"

"Neither am I," I growled back.

We both turned around to look at the light; it was there and looked as though it was still about the same distance away from us.

"You made that story up, right?"

"No, it's true; I swear, it is!"

"Let's run and see if it follows us!"

We started running, but it was still behind us, we zigzagged across the road and back, it still followed. Running off the road and into the scrub, doing massive zigzags, stopping and starting quickly, whatever we did it was still following us, and the only result of all this exercise was that we were completely knackered. It was still behind us and the same distance away. We sat down with our backs to a tree; at least sitting like that, nothing could come up from behind us. We stared at the light, it stared back at us, and neither it nor we moved. After a while, Bob, remembering the rifle, loaded it and crossing his legs placed it across them.

"We'll stay here for a bit," he said, and I, not daring to move, agreed.

The torch that we had been using flickered and died, we had no spare batteries and were left in complete blackness except for the light from the ghost who kept staring at us and we scowling back at it. Finally, we did what all teen boys do when they can't think of anything more positive, we fell asleep.

We were awoken with a start; something had made us both jump out of our skins. We checked the ghost, and it was still staring at us, but this time there was a noise, a thump, just one and then silence for perhaps thirty seconds and then another thump! I poked Bob in his ribs.

"Are you listening to that?" I whispered.

"Yeah, keep quiet," he hissed back. We sat stock still, but the thumps continued. I could take the tension no more before shouting out, "sod off, whoever you are, we're not afraid of you!" To which Bob added,

"And we're armed; we got a gun!"

"My mate is a great shot," I lied.

"Yeah, try us if you dare!"

We both stopped shouting and the echoes died away, the thumping also stopped, but the ghost was still staring at us. Everything was deathly quiet for a short while.

Thump! The same noise started again. Quickly thinking of an idea, I whispered it to Bob, and standing up, we stood back-to-back with him holding the rifle at waist height. Not being able to see in the dark, we had no idea what was going on, and we were starting to panic although neither of us wanted to show it to the other.

"We're giving you one last chance," I shouted, "then we'll open fire!"

"Okay," yelled Bob, "You've asked for it, you can't begin to understand the amount of fire-power we have here!" He must have thought that our gun had the same power as a leftover battleship from the second world war.

Fifteen dark blue gun flashes lit the night sky, each one making a roaring, deafening, almost screaming bang! Bob and I, standing back-to-back, took one small step in a circle as he fired each round, and as the final shot screamed away, we had turned a full three-hundred-and-sixty-degree circle whilst remaining back-to-back. We stood still whilst the echo of the gunshots died away and the quiet of the night returned. Whoever had been making the thumping sounds wasn't in any condition to do it again.

"Do you think we killed him?" I asked.

"I don't know, do I? Anyway, he asked for it, it was his fault, wasn't it?"

We both sat back down against the tree with our knees pulled up into our chests and were completely silent, lost in our own thoughts for a few minutes until Bob shouted at the ghost, "and if you don't go away, you'll get the same!"

If he weren't quite so scared, he'd have been in a real fighting mood.

After the silence returned, we gradually both dozed off again. Waking up as the dawn broke we noticed that the ghost had gone, and we went in search of who or whatever had been making the thumping sound.

About fifty yards from where we had been sitting, we found the culprit in the form of a dead kangaroo that had failed to take our advice from the night before! Unsure whether to hold a full Christian burial service for the poor thing we both returned and sat beneath our leafless tree feeling quite sorry for the poor animal.

Chapter Twenty-Two

After looking at the dead kangaroo, we found ourselves surprised that it hadn't hopped off when we shouted at it.

"Maybe it was transfixed by the ghost, the same as us?" suggested Bob.

"The same as you, you mean," I scoffed at him.

"Are you trying to tell me that you weren't scared?"

"Never thought about that," I lied.

"Still, it was strange though; I wonder where it went."

"To heaven or, if it was a naughty little joey, to hell; do you want to eat something?"

"I meant the ghost."

"Oh well, you should have said!"

Opening a backpack, I took the remaining lamb out and we started eating it. It was still tasty but the same as anything else; if you eat the same food every meal, it becomes boring.

"What do you miss the most?" asked Bob. I thought for a moment or two about his question before answering,

"Cheese!"

He laughed. "Cheese? We'll need to find a cow to make some of that!"

"Cows don't make cheese, people do" I giggled.

"No, but the milk from them does, doesn't it!"

"Are all you Aussies mad or just you?"

"I'm just telling you that we'd need to find a cow to make cheese."

"If I find the cow, will you promise that you'll make it jump up and down until the cheese is ready?"

"Now, who's mad?"

"Did you ever hear about that Brit and the Aussie who went fishing?"

"What Brit and Aussie?"

"Well, apparently a Brit and an Aussie went out one afternoon and decided to have a couple of cold beers. After a while, the Aussie said to the Brit, 'If I was to sneak over to your house and make wild passionate love to your wife while you were at work, and she got pregnant and had a baby, would that make us related?' The Brit, after a great deal of thought, replied, 'Well, I don't know about related, but it sure would make us even'."

"Is that supposed to be funny?" Bob asked.

"Nope, it just lets us know the difference between Brits and Aussies—the Brit is always the first to get something done!"

"Including my wife?"

"Well, someone would need to keep her happy whilst you're still learning exactly what you're supposed to be doing! Anyway, who, in their right mind, would want to marry you?"

"Ha-ha, nutter!"

We needed to move on, but after last night's experience, we were not sure if to move in the daytime or stick to our original plan and move at night. We tossed a coin and night-time won, so we waited all day for the sun to go back down before packing up our things and starting another long trudge.

Daytime quickly turned into night and we started walking. Without the torch giving us any light, our progress was awfully slow. We had hardly covered any meaningful distance but kept looking behind to see if our ghost would show itself again this evening. During one of our checks, we again spotted the light but no, wait a minute, there were two lights. Had our ghost this time brought a friend?

As we stood there watching them, the two lights came closer and were accompanied by the sound of a vehicle's engine. Immediately taking up our hitchhiking positions, we were very grateful when, in the usual big cloud of dust the vehicle came to a halt and the driver of the pickup wound down a window, asked us where we were going and told us to jump in.

We soon found out that he was the manager of a sheep station and was returning home. His home was about forty miles from where he had picked us up and he would take us as far as he could.

He was a stocky guy of average height and very chatty. During the conversation we told him of the ghost that we had seen the night before. Laughing, he stopped the pickup, and at his invitation, the three of us got out.

"You mean, that?" he asked us, pointing in the direction of our old friend.

"Yes, that's it," we replied.

"That's no ghost." He laughed even louder.

"What is it then?"

"It's the bloody moon!" His laughter slowed to a chuckle.

"The moon? That can't be the moon, can it?"

"Oh yes, it can, and yeah right, it's the moon!" He went on to tell us that in certain parts of the Australian outback and at two different times each year, the angle of the moon to the earth makes it look as though it's almost on the ground. "Nothing to be worried about." He giggled at our expense.

"We weren't worried," we lied, "it just seemed, well, strange!"

"Many strange things happen in the outback; the two of you should take extra care."

We nodded our thanks for his advice before changing the conversation and explaining that we were making our way to Darwin in the hope of jumping onto a boat to England. When asked, why, I told him that I didn't like Australia and a few other reasons. "What about Bob?" he asked.

Bob told him that he hated his mother and father so was going to the UK to start a new life without all the problems he was getting at home. "So, you're a runaway, are you?" the guy asked him.

"Sort of, I suppose, but whatever, I'm never going back there with them."

We were chatting a bit more before and in no time at all, we had arrived at the spot where the guy had to turn off to go to his sheep station.

"Are you two planning to carry on walking from here?"

"Yeah," we both answered at the same time.

"Why don't the two of you come back with me, meet Mum and have a meal with us? You can even stay the night if you want to; we've got plenty of space?"

We gladly agreed and accepted his offer. After all, the choice was either walking all night or going with the guy to his place, having a meal and somewhere to sleep. There was no argument which was the best option, and so he drove us to his home.

'Home' was a single-storey building made from a mix of bricks and wood. It had a few other buildings near it and lights were shining from the windows and doorway. A lady, about the same age as the guy, was framed in the doorway and she smiled as he introduced 'Mum' to us. Within a short time, she had prepared a really good meal for the four of us. The plates we were given were so big that I could hardly finish eating it all, but I struggled and just about made it to the end. One thing that surprised me was that here, in the middle of the outback, they had electricity, so I asked him where did they get it from?

"Right here." He laughed. "We have a generator and make our own, but it's expensive; so, we only run it a few hours at night; after that, we use paraffin lamps!" I was amazed, high tech and here in bloody Australia, who would have thought it?

"Now who wants something else to eat?" asked Mum.

"Brian is missing cheese," chipped in Bob.

"We've got plenty of that," said a smiling Mum, standing up to get some.

"Oh no, please," I answered, "I'm really full, I couldn't eat anything else!" Bob gave the same answer, and with a laugh, Mum sat down again.

"If you're both full how about we all sleep for the night, and we'll talk and eat some more in the morning," said the guy. We both nodded and he took us to the next building. "You both can sleep here, it's our sheep shearing shed! It only gets used once a year when the guys come for the sheep. It's quite warm and comfortable though."

Leaving a paraffin lamp, he wished us a good night and left us, closing the door behind him. We each made a bed using our own sleeping bags and after stripping off, settled down for the night.

"They're pretty good," said Bob.

"Yeah, but she can't be his mother, she's not old enough?"

"She's not," said Bob in his know-it-all voice, "she's his mistress!"

"So, why does he call her Mum?"

"They all do that in the outback," he replied.

"Why?"

"Because they do; can we go to sleep now?"

"Bollocks, goodnight!"

"Goodnight!"

It had been a long day, followed by a heavy meal, and within minutes, we were both out like a light.

Awake early, we got dressed and went outside. Finding a large full tank, we splashed water over our faces before going into the main house. We had tea and toast for breakfast, then went outside the house again and started to look around. There was no sign of any sheep, and personally, I think that they had got wind of Bob's shooting abilities and decided to keep away!

The outside yard didn't have much going for it either, with really nothing more than a few hand tools, an oxy-acetylene metal cutter and some metal welding equipment laying around plus, of course, the water tank that we had used earlier. Off to the right was a big billabong for storing water. We walked over and were surprised at how large it was, much, much bigger than the one we had played around in earlier. It even had a small rowing boat floating on it and tied up to the bank.

We stood there, looking at the boat when, as if from nowhere, the guy appeared and suggested that if we fancied it, we could take the boat out for a play around. Without waiting to be asked a second time, we jumped in and cast off, taking it in turns to row around the mini lake. We played around like kids and passed the next hour or so by either rowing or throwing water over each other. I thought that it was fun, but Bob really seemed in his element and confirmed that by telling me that he would love to live in a place like this. I answered him to the effect that it might be okay for a few days, but I would much rather play around back in the United Kingdom than anywhere in Australia.

When we gave up messing around with the boat and behaving like kids, we landed and tried our hands at cutting and welding metal using the equipment in the yard following the instructions given to us by the guy. Bob's cutting was better than mine, but my welding was certainly a lot tidier than the mess he ended up with.

With all the playing around the day passed very quickly, and we even went for a ride in the pickup with the guy to look at a few of the paddocks he was managing. On the way back to the house, he asked if either of us could drive, and telling him that I could but I didn't have a licence he let me drive most of the way back. Bob even showered praise by telling me that my driving was much better than he would have thought it to be without having a licence and all. I shrugged and lied to him when I said that unlike Australia, everyone in England could drive almost before they were born. I was chuffed when he believed it!

We spent the second night with the guy and his mum and in all fairness once again we had a great evening meal. It was after we had finished eating that Bob brought the question up, "What would one have to do to work on a place like this?"

"Why, are you interested?" the guy asked. Bob nodded his head.

"I could find work for the two of you here; the pay wouldn't be great but—" I stopped the guy mid-sentence.

"No, not two, just one," I interjected, "I'm going to England!"

"You can't hike through the bush on your own," said Bob, "it's too dangerous!" The guy agreed with him.

"Dangerous or not, we started this thing with the idea of going to the UK together, and with or without you, I'm going!"

"How are you going to get there on your own?"

"I can read a map as well as you can, can't I?"

The guy intervened in what was slowly beginning to turn into a row between Bob and I by saying that if I was sure I was leaving, it wouldn't be a good idea to head for Darwin. It would be much better to go back to Sydney from where, as far as he knew, the ships for the UK departed.

"And how do I get to Sydney?" I asked.

"Do you have any money?"

"Not much, but I've got some!"

"You can take the rifle and there's still the unused camera; you can sell them both," suggested Bob.

The guy then told me that if I wanted to do that, he would take me to the dirt road on which we had first met in the pickup, from there and in the daytime, it would be easy to get a lift to a place called Chinchilla and from there, a night train to Sydney.

Later when Bob and I were in the sheep shearing shed, I asked him if he was really going to stay and work on the station. He said yes, and I told him that I would leave the next morning. We wished each other good luck and I spent the night tossing and turning whilst thinking what the future had in store for me.

Chapter Twenty-Three

And so, that was that! The guy and Bob took me in the pickup to the main road and after a quick goodbye they both disappeared leaving nothing but the expected cloud of dust. I had the cine camera and rifle with me, and my first thought was to reach the nearest town and to find somewhere to sell them.

I waited, at the side of the road for perhaps two hours for a vehicle to drive past before another cloud of dust signalled that one was heading towards me. Taking up the now-familiar pose, I stuck my arm out and started to thumb a lift.

The approaching car stopped and the driver, after asking me where I was going, invited me to get in; so, putting my backpack and the rifle on the back seat, I climbed into the front passenger seat next to him. It must be said that hitchhiking in the Australian outback was a lot easier than one would have expected in so much as just about all vehicles that approached a person standing at the side of the road would almost automatically stop. I think partly out of courtesy and partly owing to the complete lack of a conventional transport system.

As we drove along, the driver asked me the usual questions and I explained my reason for being there. I was now heading for Sydney and that I needed somewhere to sell the camera and the gun. He said that would be no problem and he could help me out by showing me where I would probably get a fair price. As we were talking, he slowed down and came to a halt to allow the largest flock of sheep I had seen, or ever would see in my life, to cross the road.

Herded by men on horseback and sheepdogs, there seemed to be hundreds of thousands of the woolly creatures, all running in one long line and maybe thirty or forty animals deep. Looking at them, my thoughts returned to *Larry the Lamb* and of how he had sacrificed himself to save the life of others. We sat there stock still for maybe two hours before the way was free for us to continue with our journey. The driver explained to me that it was about time for the stations to start shearing the animals, and so the great yearly round up to get all the sheep together had begun to take place. I imagined Bob trying to round up sheep when *Larry the Ram* discovered it was Bob who'd shot his younger brother. The horns on the ram's head would play havoc with Bob's ass!

A short while later we drove through a small town and the driver stopped. After he parked his car, he signalled for me to get out and go with him into a small general store. I showed the owner of the shop the camera and the gun, and with the help of the car driver, we soon arrived at a fair price before the store owner bought both items. It seemed to me that everyone in the outback knew everyone else. Not that there were that many living out there anyway!

Feeling more relaxed and with money in my pocket plus the help of the driver who seemed to know the outback quite well, we carried on heading in the direction of the railway station. Finally arriving at the small town, with the ridiculous name of Chinchilla, my driver friend stopped the car and, after getting out, walked with me into the railway booking office.

It was starting to get dark and my driver suggested that I bought a ticket for a sleeper car on the train as then, the next day, I would arrive in Sydney feeling a little more refreshed than if I had to stay up all night in a pretty uncomfortable seat. Remembering my previous rail journey and the wooden seats I hastily agreed with his suggestion and brought the ticket that I needed. My new-found friend stayed with me on the platform, possibly thinking that someone needed to protect this bloody silly Pommie bastard until the Sydney train arrived about an hour later.

I boarded the train, said goodbye to my friend and as the train gently pulled out of the station, he wished me every success on my journey back to the United Kingdom. His comments made me feel good at least there was one person who believed that I would make it home!

The sleeper cabins on the train looked incredibly old. Mine was made of very ornate carved wood with a bunk bed against one of the carriage partitions and, as there was no one else in the cabin, I chose the bottom bunk and made myself comfortable. The train started to rattle on its long journey to Sydney and I began wondering what I would do when I arrived there.

Shortly before I had left Cardiff to travel to Australia, I had been approached by a cousin or someone like that anyway, he had the same name as me and was, by all accounts, some sort of distant family member. He had married a few months earlier and had had a separate photo album of the wedding made for relations of his living in Sydney. At that time, the cost of postage between the

United Kingdom and Australia was very high and he had asked me if I could take the album with me and either deliver it or post it, in Australia, to the family after my arrival. Drugs were virtually non-existent in those days and as there was no chance of him trying to use me to smuggle, I had willingly agreed.

The photograph album was in my suitcase which, I now suspected was waiting for me to collect at Darwin Railway Station. Nevertheless, perhaps I could kill two birds with one stone by paying them a visit to explain to them where their album was currently located and maybe there would be a small chance of them knowing where, or how, I could find and rent a room in Sydney. It was worth a try and at the very least I could tell them that I would send their photographs to them after I managed to retrieve my suitcase.

The following morning, I arrived in Sydney. I stepped off the train and asked a passer-by how I could get to the suburb of Parramatta which was the name of the district I had been given to send the photo album to. It didn't take long to find someone who gave me the directions of how to get there.

It was quite an easy ride on a local train to Parramatta, and I was quick to find the street after arriving at the local station. One thing that bothered me was that after my travels in the outback, the shirt I was wearing was grubby and it didn't seem polite to visit people whilst wearing it. So when I came across a small shop selling men's clothes I went in and looked through their shirt selection. They only had a small number and so I was not given a large choice, but I still managed to find one. Leaving the shop, I quickly took off my old shirt and pulled the new one over my head. I was now ready for the visit.

I soon found the house I was looking for and as with all houses in the street it was a single-storey detached type, with a large, unfenced garden at the front. I knocked and waited but got no answer. I knocked a few more times but still nothing. I was just about to leave when I thought I heard a noise coming from the rear of the property. Walking down the side of the house I came to a wooden garden door and the noise I had heard got louder. I realised that someone was playing in the garden. Gingerly tapping at the door, I waited, before as no one had answered my tapping, I opened it myself.

Two ladies were seated around a garden table and a little girl of around three-years of age was playing and making most of the noise that I had previously heard. None of them had heard my knocking or seen me opening the door, so I made a loud coughing noise to attract their attention.

"Excuse me," I said, walking in, "I'm looking for Mrs Robson?"

"Which one?" They asked. "We're both Mrs Robson."

"The one who is the aunt of Brian Robson, from Cardiff in Wales?" I smiled.

The oldest lady said that would be her and I introduced myself as also being Brian Robson from Cardiff but not the same one as I had mentioned earlier.

"Oh, you must be one of Ethel's grandsons?"

"Ethel?" I asked, looking, and sounding confused.

"Yes, you're young Jimmy's son, right?"

Young Jimmy? I'd never heard him called that before, but I guessed that they were referring to my father. "Yes," I answered rather lamely whilst convincing myself that it had to be my father they were talking about, as his first name was James.

I was offered a chair and sat down before I was offered a glass of orange juice whilst we carried on talking about my family members, most of whom I had never heard of. By the time they had finished asking me questions, I got the general gist that we were discussing relatives of mine from my Grangetown grans side of the family. After we had managed to sort out who was who in the family stakes, I told them about my time spent in Australia, about the photograph album and about my idea of staying in Sydney and wondering if they knew anything about how to rent a place to live.

"All in good time," my Great Aunt answered, "and you can stay here for now."

I thanked her for the offer before she asked me a rather strange question, "Where did you get that shirt you're wearing?"

Again, looking confused, I told her that I had bought it just before I visited her as the shirt, I had been wearing, was rather grubby. "What size shirt do you wear?"

"Usually, a shirt with a fourteen and a half collar size," I answered.

"What have you got on now?" Looking embarrassed, I said, "Seventeen and a half, it was the only one they had!"

She smiled a motherly smile. "Oh! You are a typical Robson, aren't you?"

121

Chapter Twenty-Four

Over the next few days, I met other members of my long-lost family including another Brian Robson who was the son of my great aunt! My family sure liked the name Brian; now there were three of us. I never did find out why the name was so popular, and I wondered exactly how many more Brian Robson's I would come across!

The new Brian worked for a company called Colonial Sugar Refineries and managed to get me a job there. The name seemed rather strange to me as, certainly on the site at which I was working, they dealt in chemicals and not sugar; I always thought the morning coffee tasted strange.

I quite liked the job, the pay wasn't too bad, and I was working completely on my own, filling up forty-four-gallon drums with some obnoxious chemical before adding a tiny, measured amount of another chemical from something that resembled a petrol pump and sealing the drums. I wasn't bothered by anyone in fact, the only other people I would see during the shift was Brian, my cousin, and a forklift driver both who would pop over occasionally. This suited me as most of the time I would pretend that I was still working in the UK.

My great aunt had prepared a bed for me on the back veranda of the house which was quite comfortable, and I spent most of my time either working or sleeping except for the weekend when Brian would take me to a horse-trotting track where I watched, and he gambled on the amazing Australian sport of horses pulling little buggies whilst trotting around the racetrack. I wasn't into horses or gambling for that matter, but it passed the time, and it was nice of him to take me with him.

One Friday evening, my great aunt told me that she had located a permanent place for me to stay and that a friend of hers had a spare room that she would make available to me. I travelled by train to the Sydney suburb of West Ride to meet the 'Joneses'.

Mr and Mrs Jones were also from Cardiff. They had two adult daughters who also lived with them and a house that was like my great aunt's. The one difference was that they had a spare bedroom. I liked the house and we chatted for a while before deciding that the next day, being Saturday, would be easy for me to move in. My room was quite nice and the food that Mrs Jones cooked was tasty and well prepared. The only problem was that Mr Jones and the two daughters worked afternoon shifts and finished work at 11 p.m. Mrs Jones didn't like being alone in the house after dark and so she used to prepare my dinner for me when I finished work, before deciding what we were going to watch on TV every evening!

She was genuinely nice and a bit motherly, but I soon got bored with watching TV every night. Not that I had anywhere to go or any friends of my own, but I never would have if I continued working alone every day and watching TV every night.

Mr Jones would work overtime on weekends and the two daughters who worked a five-day week would both go out on Saturday and Sunday evenings, that left me and Mrs Jones still watching TV. I didn't want to upset them, but something had to change.

By now I had managed to save a little money, and I went to the local railway station and arranged for my suitcase to be sent from Darwin to West Ride railway station, it would be nice to have all my clothes back again. The case arrived a few days later, and after collecting it, I arranged all my clothes in the wardrobe of my room, before going over to my great aunt's where I took the photo album, I had promised to get back for her. On the way over I brought a box of chocolates and a bunch of flowers for her as a way of saying thank you for the help she had given me.

I had kept the telephone number of the sheep station where Bob was working and one evening, I decided to phone him. He was happy to hear from me and I could tell by his voice that he was not happy working there. I told him all that had happened to me since we last met, where I was living and that I had a job, before he blurted out how much he hated sheep and sheep stations. Before the money had run out in the call box, he asked me if I could help him come to Sydney to live. Telling him that I didn't know if I could arrange that, but that I would try to find out, I agreed that I would phone him again a few days later.

Walking back down the street from the phone box I weighed up the pros and the cons of having Bob living here and, by the time I had reached the Joneses' house, I had made up my mind.

Mrs Jones and I were, as usual, sitting down watching the television when I broached the subject.

"Do you remember my friend Bob, the one I told you about?"

"Yes, dear," she answered.

"Well, I telephoned him earlier this evening and he's thinking of moving to Sydney but will need somewhere to stay." She nodded her head.

"I was wondering if you would let him stay here. He could always share my room, and his rent would give you extra money each week?" I looked to gauge her reaction before I continued, "also, I get bored; it would be nice to have someone else for company."

She thought for a moment before speaking, "Let me speak to Mr Jones, but I don't see any problem!" After that we went back to watching television.

The next morning as I was leaving for the sugar factory that secretly produced chemicals, Mrs Jones with a smile, said, "It's okay. I spoke to Mr Jones, and your friend can stay here!" I was quite pleased, and as I caught the train to travel the four stops to where I was working, I started making plans. Even better news was awaiting me when I arrived at work as I was informed that the following Monday was a public holiday—National Kangaroo Day or something like that—and we all had an extra day off work!

That evening, I phoned Bob and told him what I had arranged. He was over the moon and even happier when I told him that as I had a long weekend coming up I would travel to Queensland to meet with him. We arranged that he would hitchhike from the sheep station and we would meet in Charleville the following Saturday and travel back to Sydney the same day. Talking it over with Mr Jones, he advised me that the quickest way would be to catch a train to Brisbane Friday evening, change trains and travel to meet Bob, then leave as soon as possible and both travel back the same way. I should then be in time for work on Tuesday morning. I set my travel plans, but at that time, I didn't realise that Mr Jones had no more of an idea about travel in Australia than I did!

The following Friday I finished my shift at work and, after rushing home to collect my bag, I quickly made my way to Sydney's railway station and caught the Brisbane train. The journey was comfortable enough and the night passed quickly. As soon as I arrived in Brisbane and to avoid wasting time, I went to the booking office and asked what time the next train to Charleville was?

"10 o'clock" was the reply.

"10 a.m., or 10 p.m.?" I asked.

"10 a.m.", then after a brief pause, "next Wednesday!"

"You're joking, right?" He shook his head, and I could see by the look on his face that he was deadly serious.

"I've got to be there today," I said feeling dismayed.

"Try Ansett ANA" was his stone-faced reply.

Ansett ANA was the Australian domestic airline that I had flown on from Sydney to Melbourne when I first arrived in Australia. It appeared that now I had no choice but to fly with them again! I went to their office and was relieved to hear that they flew to Charleville every other day and that today was one of those 'other' days. There was also a return flight to Brisbane at 11 a.m. the following morning. The days and times fitted in with my plans, but when I asked the cost of the fare it didn't fit in at all! I simply didn't have enough money. After carefully thinking, I asked if they would accept a cheque and found myself buying a ticket to fly to my choice of destinations. Armed with the ticket I went to the airport and after checking that the plane was on time, I phoned Bob.

We had earlier arranged that he would wait at the railway station and that if I had any problem, I should phone the railway station and ask for him—when I phoned, he was waiting there, and I informed him of the change of plans and that our meeting place would now be the airport.

Apart from the old propeller plane rattling and shaking around my flight was quite uneventful, I had developed quite a lot of sympathy for the stewards and stewardesses who risked their lives daily flying in those old contraptions. Landing on a dirt runway, we taxied in a cloud of the usual dust to an old wooden building, and as I exited the plane, the first thing I saw was the grinning face of Bob.

We went into town, and after sitting down we started chatting and went through all that we had done in the past and how we both saw our futures. He asked me if I still wanted to go back to the UK and I said that was one hundred per cent certain; the only question was when and how! I also told him that I had to be in work on Tuesday morning, and the only way to do that was to catch another plane leaving the next day as there was no train until the middle of the week plus it would take too long, making me late for work.

After finding an old hotel near the railway station we rented a room for the night. Bob, after deciding he needed a shower, went into the bathroom, and came back telling me that the bathroom drains were stinking. I told him that it reminded me of the rest of Australia anyway; he still picked up enough courage to shower and, on his return, I commented that was one less smell. We both laughed and decided that we would go for a walk to pass away some of the time.

After walking for a while, we found a place to eat and, as we carried on looking around the small town, came across a Catholic Church. We stopped when, much to my surprise, Bob suggested that we go inside.

"For what?" I asked.

"To ask God to forgive us?" he answered in a serious voice.

"Forgive us for what?"

"I don't know, all the dud cheques, maybe?"

The thought of asking God for a favour didn't impress me one little bit, after all he must have had some hand in getting me into this mess in the first place. I suggested that he went into the church by himself and that I'd wait for him. He was gone for about ten minutes; he must have confessed to quite a lot or perhaps he dealt with each cheque separately!

After he had returned, we went off laughing and joking to the Ansett ANA office and booked two tickets to Sydney via Brisbane for the following day. Bob could ask God to forgive us for that cheque the next time they spoke!

We had a restful night, before we returned to the airport the next day and flew to Brisbane, then after we had disembarked from the first plane, we boarded a flight to Sydney. As the flight progressed, a stewardess came around with a drinks trolley and, knowing the drinks were free I asked Bob if he fancied one?

"A drink of what?" he asked.

"I don't know, I don't usually drink either, well not much anyway, so take a guess at something!"

"I don't drink either," he said.

"Well, they won't have milkshakes up here, so we'd better pick on something else."

We settled for a gin and tonic each and sat back living the hi-so life or so we thought at the time!

Chapter Twenty-Five

Things changed for the better in West Ride after Bob moved in. After he arrived back, he had been introduced to the Joneses and everyone was getting on like a house on fire. On the Tuesday I went back to work and arrived there on time whilst Bob started hunting around looking for a job. He soon found one and we were both pleased that he was working the same hours as myself, so giving us plenty of time to mess around after work.

Instead of watching television every night, the two of us sat outside on the steps of the house in the warm evening air and just chatted about the day's work or told each other some crazy jokes. Mrs Jones was quite happy as well; she still had her television in the evenings, yet she still wasn't alone as we were always on call from a few feet away. Sometimes after chatting, we would join her in the house and either talk with her or all three would watch some TV. Things were getting on great; that was until one evening when I suggested to Bob that we could go over and see my Great Aunt Mrs Robson.

Oh, it wasn't Mrs Robson and Bob meeting each other that was the problem in fact, that worked out quite well; the problem was that she had another visitor, and he knew that my one ambition was to get back to the United Kingdom.

We spent about an hour talking with my aunt and her visitor, and the whole conversation was based around the fact that in a few days he was returning home to, of all places, Cardiff! The more he talked the unhappier I became. What gave him the right to go back when I couldn't? Sure, he'd lived in Australia for about four years, and sure, he'd saved up the boat fare and had a passport, but in my mind, it still didn't make it right! He was doing something that I desperately wanted to do.

He was going and I had to stay here for two years or pay the Australian government both my fare out and then pay my fare back to the UK and, to top it all off, the British government wouldn't even issue me a passport until the time had passed or I managed to pay out all the money. It wasn't as though I even liked it here, I hated the place! The more he spoke the more I wished the boat he was travelling on would sink!

After an hour, I'd put up with enough of listening to the visitor whose name was Jack and I decided to leave. Bob and I said goodbye to my great aunt and were almost out the house when Jack asked what we were doing the following evening.

"Not going to the UK, that's for sure!" I replied.

He laughed before telling us that he had an idea and that if we were free, he'd like to come and visit us. Before I had a chance to answer him with an abrupt 'no way', Bob had said yes and the two of them arranged that we would all meet at our place the next day.

The following day I went to work, and the previous evening's fiasco gradually slipped from my mind. It wasn't until after returning home that evening that I was reminded by Bob of the impending visit. Almost as soon as he had mentioned it, Mrs Jones who hadn't heard Bob's comment piped in, "are you two expecting a visitor this evening?"

"Yes, my aunt's friend Jack is supposed to be coming over, how do you know that?"

"Your aunt phoned me earlier today and said I was to warn you both not to listen to or take any notice of him."

"I told you; I knew he was mad," I said to Bob.

"She didn't say if he was mad or not, she just said to be careful," replied Mrs Jones, looking slightly put out at my suggestion that our forthcoming visitor might be a madman, and a madman who was originally from Wales no less!

Jack was around fifty years of age and apparently not liked by many people. He had been in Australia about four years and had held many jobs. I never did find out why people didn't like him I only knew that if he turned up that evening, there was no way I was going to listen to his bragging about going to the UK. Bob, on the other hand, was more interested in getting to the bottom of what this idea, that Jack had mentioned earlier, entailed.

We were both sitting on the front steps of the house when Jack, the self-made man of the moment, turned up. He greeted us and we returned the greeting before he sat down alongside us. After a little, completely non-consequential chat and my wish to cut the visit short, I cut to the chase.

"So, Jack, what can we do for you?" I asked, wondering how he would broach the idea of borrowing some money.

"It's not what you can do for me, it's more what I can do for you!"

"You do something for us?" asked Bob in surprise.

"Yes, you both want to go to the UK, right?" Before Bob could answer, I chipped in with a curtly sounding question, "So what! Why do you keep bringing that subject up?"

Ignoring my question, he asked, "Have you ever thought of stowing away?" Stowing away? This suggestion piqued my interest and my irritation toward him waned a little.

"And how exactly are we supposed to do that?"

"Oh God, you're not thinking too quickly, are you?" he said. "What's wrong with the 'Southern Cross' and my helping you out!"

The 'Southern Cross' was, in 1963, a twenty-one-thousand-ton liner that carried around one thousand two hundred passengers between the United Kingdom and Australia with the same number of passengers on its return journey. By chance, it just so happened to be the ship that was going to take Jack back home in the next few days. Sarcastically, I asked him, "We just turn up, and they invite us on board; no tickets and no passports, right?"

"No, idiot, I have three visitor passes for people who want to come and see me off. I give them to you, you board as visitors and forget to leave when the ship sails."

"And they're not going to notice us walking around the deck with a suitcase for the next thirty or forty days whilst we all merrily sail to England?"

He made a tutting kind of sound with his lips before saying, "I take your suitcases on board with mine, and you two stay in my cabin until we get there!" He seemed sincere with his answer which made me more than interested.

"And you'd do that for us?" I asked, getting even more involved in his idea.

"Yes, if you don't tell anyone it was me who helped you." "Dib-dib scout's honour," I replied before laughing at the idea that we would tell anyone.

We chatted a bit longer before I agreed that we could take advantage of Jack's offer and head back to the UK on the ship. Another half an hour past and we had agreed that we would meet him at Sydney's Circular Quay, complete with suitcases, on the day of the ship's sailing. He gave us two of the visitors' passes that he had with him. These unbelievably valuable pieces of paper would allow us on the boat to say goodbye to him and were also a particularly important part of his devious plan and proof that Jack was serious about the whole idea.

Circular Quay was part of Sydney harbour. Located near the harbour bridge, it was the place where all the large passenger ships arrived and departed to various international destinations including the UK. I was elated with Jack's unusually generous offer and the thought of going home, but Bob didn't seem quite so happy about it.

Jack left us to make his way home, leaving Bob and I to have a long chat. It was immediately obvious that Bob didn't want to go along with the plan. He made up all sorts of excuses, with the most important being that he didn't have a passport and even if it worked and we arrived in the UK, they wouldn't let him stay. I countered that argument by reminding him that I didn't have a passport either! He said that me not having one didn't count as they couldn't throw me out as I was British. If Bob went or not was up to him, but I wasn't going to miss the chance of getting back home.

Finishing our conversation, we went back indoors where Mrs Jones had been waiting to poke her nose in and find out what Jack had wanted. I told her that he had an idea to borrow some money but knowing that he was going back to the UK, we had told him no. She seemed quite pleased with that answer and told us both that we had been incredibly wise.

The day of the ship's sailing had arrived, and after I had packed my suitcase, Bob helped me smuggle it through the bedroom window and out of the house. I didn't say anything to the Joneses as I knew that they wouldn't agree and would try and prevent it from happening. As agreed, Bob would go with me to where the boat was docked and later, after I was safely stowed away, he would explain everything to the Joneses and then continue to carry on living there.

We arrived at Circular Quay and, sure enough, Jack was waiting for us as we had arranged. He took my suitcase from me and said that he would get it on board. I told him that Bob would not be coming with us, and so he would only have to put me up in his cabin. This didn't seem to worry him, and it was arranged that after the ship had left port, I was to knock on his cabin door, and he would help get things organised for me.

Bob and I were both relieved that Jack had met us as planned. We had both felt sure that he wouldn't keep his promise, but after the meeting that morning, we felt that he could be trusted and that we had been wrong to distrust him in the first place. I had mixed feelings at that time as I was sorry to leave Bob behind but extremely excited at the prospect of departing from Australia.

It was time for me to board the ship, and as Bob had declined to come on board the boat to say his goodbyes, we said farewell on the quayside. I told him that I was glad that we had met, and I would write to him after I got back home. He, in turn, told me that I was the best Pommie he had ever known, and he would miss me.

After shaking hands with him, I turned around and walked up the boarding ramp, offering my visitor's pass to the crew member standing there. I was incredibly happy but somewhat scared to be invited aboard. Never having been on a ship before I was uncertain what to do, so I aimlessly wandered around for a while until the ship's loudspeaker system started asking all visitors to please make their way ashore as the ship was about to sail. My stomach felt as if it was full of knots, and although I, in a way, felt very happy at simply being on board, the ship made me feel as though I had already left Australia, the other part of me was terrified as to what was going to happen next.

After two or three reminders to visitors to leave the ship they eventually made the final announcement and started playing the only decent song ever to come out of the British Commonwealth Country of Australia: *Waltzing Matilda*. With the strains of *The jolly swagman, camping by a billabong* and the boats horn making loud horn blowing noises the ship with the aid of tugboats, slowly started to move away from the quay. The land side of the deck was crowded with passengers, most of whom were leaning over the ship's rail and waving goodbye to their loved ones. Rather than stand out like a sore thumb I joined them and waved goodbye to Australia but, search as I may, I couldn't spot Bob who must have already left the docks.

Within an hour and under the ships own steam we were heading out of Sydney harbour and under the harbour bridge, another hour, and we would be in the open sea.

Most of the passengers had by now disappeared from the deck and, I suppose, returned to their cabins so, after taking a seat on deck I started to relax. I would wait a while before finding out where Jack's cabin was located and giving him an afternoon knock.

It was quite a sunny day, but there must be a storm due as the ship seemed to be swaying from side to side a bit, and to be honest, my stomach didn't feel too good. I had watched the pilot leave the ship in a little black and white boat and thought how brave he must be to tackle the waves in something so small. Watching the sea had made me giddy and feeling a little nauseous, so I sat down far enough from the side of the ship that I couldn't see the water. Forty days of feeling like this didn't sound too exciting a prospect to me, however the thought of arriving at Southampton or some other such port in the UK cheered me up no end.

I put up with the sickly feeling for about an hour before picking up enough courage to stand up and starting on a quick tour of the ship. I soon found the ship's inquiry desk and asked them for the number of Jack's cabin. They looked it up and told me, plus gave me directions as to how to find it. Half staggering, half walking, I made my way there and knocked on the door. It was opened by Jack himself who, putting his finger up to his lips, whispered that he would meet me on the deck. I nodded, told him where I would be and returned to my deck chair from where the sea was not visible.

Jack arrived about five minutes after I had sat down and after informing me that I didn't look too good, he gave me the rest of the bad news. "You can't stay in my cabin," he said.

"Why the hell not, you said that you'd arrange it?" I said somewhat in disbelief.

He started blabbering on that there were eight people in the cabin and that when he had suggested it to me, he didn't realise that there would be so many.

"Just go and tell them; tell them I only need a small space on the floor!" The idiot refused to do it and after a short shouting match, I asked what I was supposed to do now? He just said that he didn't know but that there was nothing he could do about it and that I would have to find some way to help myself. I was right in the first place; he was an idiot!

Jack and I separated, and I remained seated on the deck with my mind split between two pressing subjects. The first was where I would be able to hide for the next forty days and the second thought danced around the idea of whether I could prevent myself from vomiting over the next forty minutes.

The rolling of the boat had to take priority as the giddiness and dry stomach heaving became worse. The problem at sea is that there is nowhere to hide with the whole boat moving; there was simply nowhere to go and it felt like being on a fast-moving merry-go-round, feeling sick, yet unable to step off!

I had been sitting there feeling as I was going to puke for only a short time but, which seemed to me to be an eternity or even a lifetime, when I first noticed the man dressed in a ship's uniform standing next to me.

"You're looking a bit pale," he said smiling, "are you feeling okay?"

"I would be if the ship stopped moving," I managed to reply before vomiting all over the place.

"Oh, dear", he said before adding. "Let's get you to the sickbay."

He helped me to stand up and allowed me more time to vomit yet again. Then, with his assistance, I walked to get medical help. Once in the sickbay I vomited a few more times (this time down the toilet), splashed my face with cold water and then sat down still feeling giddy. For those readers who have never experienced the joy of seasickness—it is akin to that of drinking too much alcohol with the only difference being that whilst you are feeling as if you are dying, you can't stop drinking and promise yourself that you will never do it again. Seasickness can be compared to feeling drunk and vomiting whilst continuing to drink!

As helpful as the doctor in the sickbay was, I couldn't face the prospect of lying down or standing up and defiantly not of sitting down. In other words, I just felt in a complete mess with nowhere to go to stop the moving of the ship!

After a few more vomiting sessions, the doctor gave me some medicine in tablet form which seemed to stop my wanting to share my lunch with everyone else on board. A few more tablets and the giddiness stopped, or at least, stayed at a tolerable level. I seemed to be making a full recovery and I apologised to the man in the uniform and the doctor for causing so much trouble. "If only the sea wasn't so rough." I gasped.

"Rough? There's not even a swell." They both laughed. "It's as flat as a millpond!" I judged from that comment that when I was younger, it was just as well that I never joined the merchant navy.

The doctor prescribed a few more of the tablets with the advice to take one in the morning and another at night for the next day or so before producing something resembling a logbook. "What's your name and cabin number?" he asked.

"My name's Brian; I forget the cabin number," I lied.

"No problem, what's your surname?"

"Robson," I answered before it suddenly dawned on me that I should have given Jack's details. Since I thought that I was dying, I hadn't been thinking straight and dropped myself right in it. No sooner had my travels started than it was over, and the game was up.

The ship's captain was a man of perhaps sixty years of age with a grey goatee beard and, looking just as much of a ship's captain as you could possibly imagine. He was staring at me. With him was the man in the uniform who had taken me to the sickbay and other ship's officers who were all carrying out various duties connected with their working on the bridge of the ship.

"Does anyone else know that you are aboard?" the captain growled.

I shook my head and lied. As I said no, I wondered why I was lying to save Jack's skin after all he had done absolutely nothing for me. Making a huffing sound before speaking, the captain continued, "We should throw you overboard!" Believing what he said, I quickly decided that, as I couldn't swim well, that the idea would not be in my best interest and so I started trying to enthral him with various ideas as to why I should get back to the UK. I ended with the suggestion that I could work my passage back and that I would be prepared to do any job he felt suitable for my immense talents. "Impossible," he answered, "the same as stowing away, it's against the law for us to offer you a job!" I tried a new tactic.

"How about I become a passenger and you give me time to pay the fare later?" That didn't seem to be working either and it wasn't long before I was completely out of any ideas.

Actually, a few years before, I had watched the film *Mutiny on the Bounty*, and as the thoughts of being flogged by a 'cat-of-nine tails' didn't really appeal to me I deemed it better to keep my mouth shut.

The captain nodded his head at one of the men in a uniform who, after nodding back to him, took me from the bridge of the ship down to the boats lock up. It was a small empty room, containing nothing except a bed, and had a lockable steel door as the entrance. He opened the door and politely invited me to step inside. I followed his instructions, and the door banged shut.

Lying down on the bed with my arms folded behind my head, I pondered my options. It didn't take me long to conclude that I didn't have any, so I took the easy way out and as usual fell asleep.

About thirty minutes later that I was woken up by a lot of shouting and banging from outside the door. I was considering making a complaint to room service when the door burst open and the same officer who took me down there told me to get out of the room. Thinking the ship was sinking, I didn't need a second telling before I quickly nipped outside. A group of officers from the bridge were grappling with two men in civilian clothing who were fighting them back and who they were trying to throw into the now-empty room. After a minute or two, they succeeded in their task and quickly locked the door. An officer then informed me that today was my lucky day, I interrupted him with a cheeky grin and said, "You're taking me to the UK?"

"Wishful thinking," he laughed before adding, "but I am going to give you the complete run of the ship!"

He went on to tell me that they only had one holding cell and the two guys, who were also stowaways, were causing problems whereas I, being as pure as the driven slush, had been well behaved. The men would be locked up and I would have my freedom with only one condition being that I would have to agree to. When the ship entered the port of Wellington New Zealand, which was its first port of call, I would have to go and find the officer and then we would decide what to do next. I willingly agreed and was given a nice cabin, and as he promised, the complete run of the ship!

It took four days to get to Wellington, and although the main reason for the journey was to escape from Australia, I must admit to having a good time. I enjoyed it so much that I would recommend that anyone wishing to stow-away from Australia use the services of the 'Southern Cross'. For those seriously contemplating it, don't bother, as the ship was scrapped in 2002.

For those four days I could go anywhere I wanted on the ship and was able to mix with either the passengers or the crew whichever, at the time, I fancied doing. Most however was spent in the crew's quarters and I found myself getting on well with them. They had meals that were the same as the passenger's food and the buffet section of the canteen was very well supplied. The crew worked shifts that were four hours on and four hours off and during the day, I used to find where my new-found friends were working and join them for a while to have a cosy chat. Most evenings were spent in the crew lounge where they held regular parties and played a game known as 'crown and anchor'. This was a game that involved throwing a dice which had both a crown and an anchor printed on it; the game was easy to play, and I joined in with them most of the time.

Whenever I got the chance, I tried to persuade the officers to talk to the captain, who they all called 'the old man', and to try and get me permission to work my way to the UK. They explained that it was not worth trying to persuade him and, in any case, it was virtually impossible; he would never agree, as it was completely against the company rules.

All good things come to an end and soon the four days were over, as in the early hours of the morning, we sailed into Wellington Harbour. Keeping my promise, I unwillingly found the officer with whom I had made the deal to surrender and told him that I was keeping my part of the deal. He seemed quite surprised that he didn't have to come looking for me and we sat down over a cup of tea while he explained that after we docked, they would put me ashore and they wouldn't make any criminal charges against me. I should not try and get back on board or they might look at the whole thing from a different light. He also said that he and other members of the crew were sorry that they couldn't let me stay on board until we reached Southampton, but rules were rules, and it was impossible. I asked if I could go and say goodbye to the friends I had made whilst on board and he told me that it wouldn't be a problem, just come and find him again, when I had finished chatting with them.

After leaving him I went straight to the passenger section and knocked on Jack's cabin door. We both went up on deck, and in no uncertain terms, I told him that after we docked, I had to leave the ship. Sarcastically thanking him for breaking his promise I made sure that he understood that I wanted my suitcase back and that he had better get it off and return it to me or I might just tell the captain exactly how I managed to get on board in the first place. Unsure if I would or wouldn't stick to my threat, he immediately agreed to meet me at midday at the entrance to the port.

Going back to the crew section of the ship I met up with three or four lads who I had got to know well and who seemed devastated that I was going to be dumped and not taken back to the UK. Telling me that the ship's captain was himself going ashore for a few days, they invited me to join with them to wish him farewell. I was in no mood to wish him anything, but although I tried to make excuses, they insisted that I went with them.

The customs' checkpoint at the port was located more or less on the same level as the deck of the ship that was used to embark and disembark, and the lads stopped just a few yards from that point and leant on the ship's rail overlooking the customs area. You could quite clearly see and hear what the customs officers were doing or saying as the slightest sound would echo around the area. It wasn't long before the ship's captain with his overnight bag walked down the gangplank and stopped in front of a customs officer before offering his bag for inspection.

"How long are you going for?" the customs man asked in a friendly voice.

"Only two days," jovially replied the Captain.

"Did you pack the bag yourself and is everything in it yours?"

The Captain nodded his head just as the customs guy unzipped the bag. Once again, the Captain nodded his head, and the customs officer withdrew his hand from the bag and held up two pairs of ladies' knickers!

"Do you always wear these?" asked a smiling officer.

The Captain, looking extremely embarrassed, tried to explain that the knickers didn't belong to him, but the customs man was having none of it.

"You just said that everything in the bag was yours," he commented with a wink and a grin before zipping the bag back up and handing it back to the Captain who made a hasty departure from the area whilst looking even more embarrassed and not knowing quite where to look. Had he have glanced back at his ship he would have seen the four seamen and me still leaning on the rail with big smiles covering half our faces.

"Does he wear knickers?" I asked the lads.

"No, we planted them in the bag," answered the one.

"And that'll teach him a lesson," replied another!

We all had a good laugh as I wished them good luck, and after telling them that when they arrived back home to give my best wishes to the UK, I reported back to the ship's officer.

Later that day, I was put ashore in Wellington by the same officer who had helped me on my sea voyage and who then left me to my own devices. I hung around until midday, met up with Jack, got my suitcase back and then gave some thought as to what I was going to do next.

Chapter Twenty-Six

Wellington was not just a new city to me but was also located in a new Country and to be honest, I knew absolutely nothing about either the Country or the City! The thought of being here on my own didn't exactly excite me; in fact, it had the opposite effect and scared me to death. Even Sydney seemed a much friendlier place as at least I knew people there and had somewhere to live. I dragged my suitcase behind me for a while, unsure of where to go or what to do, until I made a beeline for somewhere that I had learnt a lot about whilst living in Australia.

Wellington's main railway station was only a few hundred yards from the entrance to the port, and so I went there, sat down on a bench, and tried to work out my next move.

The time ticked on, but as hard as I tried to think, I couldn't come up with any good ideas to save my soul. Eventually, bored and with no idea what to do, I caught a commuter train and went on a local trip. The train travelled past some of the most breath-taking scenery I had ever seen. After going through the suburbs of Wellington, the train started to climb up the hills that surrounded the city, and soon we were high above sea level. We were heading to a place called Upper Hutt which is a small township not too far outside of Wellington. To get there we travelled midway between the mountain peaks towering high above us and the ocean far below. We were travelling on a strip of land that looked as if it had been carved out of the rock face. The views were stunning, and even for someone like me, who thought that he had all the worries in the world placed on his shoulders, couldn't help but just sit back and feel amazed at the scenery.

It wasn't too long before my trip was over, and as I returned to Wellington Railway Station the sky was darkening as night-time descended. I started to think of how to find somewhere to sleep for the night. Local trains, which were equipped with automatic doors, were pulling into the platforms; the drivers turning off their lights and, as I suddenly noticed, leaving the doors open. This was an obvious choice of accommodation for the night and so, when no one was looking, I sneaked aboard a local train and settled down to wait out the darkness.

I spent a fitful night trying to sleep without having too much success. I just spent the night tossing and turning, sitting up and laying down until the dawn finally broke. Not wanting to find myself caught on the train when it left the station to start its journey later that day. I stepped off quite early and just wandered around on the platform trying to waste the time. The suitcase I was carrying was a big problem as it was too heavy to carry around with me all day and so, as soon as it opened, I checked it into the station left-luggage office and took a slow walk to nowhere.

My walk took me back to the port, the only place in Wellington that I knew and as I walked past the entrance, I bumped into some of my old seafaring mates, who were returning to the 'Southern Cross' which was about to sail for its next destination later that day.

I chatted with them for a while and told of my predicament and of how I only had a few Aussie pounds left with no idea of what to do. Their first suggestion was that they would smuggle me back on board the ship and hide me away until we reached the UK.

As much as I liked that idea, I turned it down and told them that if I got caught a second time I would be in deep trouble. They suggested that the only other alternative was for me to go to the 'Catholic Seamen' Mission' and throw myself at the mercy of the priest who operated it. Telling them that it might be a problem as I wasn't either a seaman or a Catholic, they advised me to explain that I had stowed away and to do the same as everyone else about being Catholic; if asked, just lie!

Later that day, with a heavy heart, I watched as the 'Southern Cross' left port and sailed into the blue beyond. As the ship continued its journey, I told myself that now I was homeless, stateless, jobless, knowledge less, almost moneyless, and friendless!

After one last wave to the ship, I managed to find the Mission's address and made my way, half-heartedly, to the place. Not expecting too much I managed to locate the priest and sat down with him for a long chat. I told him my whole sorry story and that my aim was to get back to the United Kingdom. He listened to all I had to say before telling me that the only help he was able to offer was a few days of free food and a bed for the night on his sofa. I thanked him and accepted the offer before he asked me if my friends in Australia knew where I was. I told him that I didn't know but that it was unlikely that they would have any idea of my current whereabouts. Smiling, he told me that one of the other services he could offer me, if I gave him the Joneses telephone number, was to contact them and let them know where I was. This would help as if for no other reason than to set their minds at rest. I gave him the number and then at his suggestion I went off to collect my suitcase and bring it back to the Mission.

After retrieving the suitcase, I returned to where the Holy Father was waiting for me; he had a smile on his face and seemed genuinely happy to see me again. As soon as I sat down, he explained that he had phoned the Joneses in Sydney who had been quite shocked to hear that I was in New Zealand and had offered to lend me the airfare to return to Australia. On my behalf he had accepted their offer and a ticket was currently being arranged for me to travel. That night, I slept in the Mission and the following morning, I went to the office of Air New Zealand to collect my ticket back to Sydney. The Mission's priest arranged my trip to the airport and barely one week after leaving Australia I was on my way back to the place that I had been so glad to leave.

It is interesting to note that in those days people didn't require passports or any other documents to travel back and forth between New Zealand and Australia so, boarding the plane was quite easy and straightforward. I spent a very unhappy time on the aircraft trying to work out what I was going to say to the Joneses when I got back.

After the plane landed in Sydney, I made my way to West Ryde still feeling very anxious as to what I was going to say. Arriving at the Joneses' front door, I gingerly knocked and was pleased when it was opened by Bob. He had a big smile on his face, a smile which grew even larger when I whispered to him that I had no idea what was going to happen!

"Don't worry about a thing" was his answer. "They know it was all Jack's fault", he had told them the story and arranged everything for my return.

Mrs Jones seemed pleased to see me and told me that if I had followed her advice, I would never have listened to Jack in the first place. I was happy enough to agree with her and let the matter rest.

We spent the rest of the evening with me enthralling them about my stow-away episode, my experience on the ship and what it was like in New Zealand. In one way, it was good to be back as at least I had a bed to sleep in. However, for all the promises I made that night, one failure at getting home was not going to stop me from trying again!

I was pleased to find that for some reason my job at the chemical plant had been kept open for me and so the following morning I sheepishly returned to work only to find that other employees were smiling and asking me if I felt better. From those comments, I gathered that I had been ill so, whilst thanking them for their concern, I carried on filling the forty-gallon drums just as if nothing untoward had happened.

Chapter Twenty-Seven

Things had pretty much returned to normal in West Ryde. After a few weeks I had returned the money lent by the Jones family for my airfare. I continued to go to work then, as usual, either sat on the front steps chatting to Bob or watching television with Mrs Jones. All we talked about was how much I detested Australia and how I was planning to do something again to get home.

In truth, I had no idea how I was going to achieve this feat, but the chatting gave me ideas to dream about later each night.

One evening, Bob came back from work and intimated that he needed to speak with me urgently. Not wanting Mrs Jones to listen in I nodded my head in the direction of the front steps and we both went to our usual meeting place. Bob looked worried and I couldn't wait to ask him what the problem was. Finally, he told me that the police had paid a visit to his workplace, and whilst confused I asked him what did that have to do with us? "Those cheques," he gushed back. "I think it might have been about the cheques!"

To be honest, I had completely forgotten about them, but his urgent-sounding voice brought the whole stupid thing back to life. I kept asking him if he was sure the police visit was about us, and for some illogical reason, he was positive. What were we going to do? If they had found out it was us and where he was working, it wouldn't take them long to discover where we were living. Bob suggested that, as we were the modern-day equivalent of the Ned Kelly gang, the entire Australian police force were probably out looking for us and perhaps we should go to the main police station with our hands held high and surrender so avoiding another shoot-out as had happened to that law abiding young man! I vetoed this idea on the grounds that the Kelly gang never surrendered, and neither would we. They could come and get us! Quite apart from coming to get us, as it was still rush hour in Sydney, they would be busy controlling traffic.

One idea was that we could board the house up and arm ourselves with deadly weapons, but what if they never came or didn't turn up on time? We'd need to stock up on food and prepare for a long siege, but even that idea had its drawbacks. Mrs Jones would surely realise that something was going on and we didn't want her to know the sordid details. We needed to disappear, and the sooner the better at least, that was Bob's idea. Luckily, for us, it was a Friday and so we'd both just been paid from work; now was the ideal time to do it. We went back into the house and Bob, after explaining to Mrs Jones that he was going out that evening, retired to the bedroom under the pretence of making himself look pretty, and packed his bag and my suitcase. I sat with her as she happily told me that she and I would have a wonderful night watching television.

After packing our bags Bob opened the bedroom window and dropped it all outside onto the grass strip at the side of the house, before coming back into the lounge and telling Mrs Jones and I that he was off out. After saying goodbye, he left the room and went around to the side of the property where he collected our entire luggage, and after moving it onto the pavement, he waited for me to join him.

After a few minutes, I made some excuse for going into the bedroom before returning to the lounge with Bob's empty wallet. I told Mrs Jones that he had forgotten his money before racing outside under the pretence of returning it to him. Within minutes and each carrying our own property we were both on our way to the railway station.

Once again, we travelled up north to Queensland with for some reason the crazy idea of reaching Darwin still etched in our minds. Arriving at our new destination we left the train and reverted to the by-now well-rehearsed plan of hitchhiking. The main difference between this and our last time was that apart from a waterproof sheet that we had managed to obtain, we had little by way of camping equipment. We slept under the sheet at night whilst during the day we were eating in any small or cheap café that we managed to come across.

In those days, kangaroo hunting was a favoured occupation for those living in the outback. The hunting was mainly centred around one of the many small towns lucky enough to accommodate a branch of a company that was rich enough to install an abattoir with a large freezer. Companies would employ 'kangaroo-shooters'. Men or boys, who, at night, would travel in the back of pickup trucks armed with a bright spotlight and various arrays of guns. The driver would locate one of the many packs of kangaroos and then switch on the truck's light beam. The animals would stand stock still staring into the light whilst the 'roo-shooters' would annihilate as many of the animals as possible. Once the pickup was full of the dead carcasses, the driver drove at breakneck speed to the local abattoir where the night's kill was processed before being placed in the large freezers to be picked up the following day by articulated freezer trucks. They were then transported to Brisbane and turned into pet-foods! Over the years, the Aussies very nearly wiped out the kangaroo population until legislation was finally introduced to stop the slaughter.

Shooting these kangaroos was a rough existence and was just as dangerous for the hunter as it was for the hunted. With the rough terrain, it was not unheard of for the pickups, whilst at speed chasing their prey, to overturn and land on top of the occupants who were travelling in the rear of the truck.

Quite apart from overturning trucks, 'Roos' that had been shot but not killed could prove extremely dangerous adversaries. Stunned by a bullet, the animal would appear to be dead but would return to life when approached by the hunters. Lashing out with its tail or razor-sharp claws it could soon take a man down. Beginners such as Bob and I were even more susceptible as it took quite some time to get used to this dirty business and to be told to load the 'hopefully' dead animals whilst putting up with all the shouting and activity from the guys whose full-time job it was to kill them.

Surprisingly, the shooters were welcomed by the locals and farmers in the area as a way of culling the many herds of kangaroos running wild and destroying crops and property.

Bob and I joined one of these 'roo-shooting' teams where we helped to hunt the animals and were paid a pittance, the amount depending on the number of animals slaughtered. We slept under our waterproof sheet during the day and worked during the night. After two successive nights we had both had had enough of it and, after collecting our miserable pittance we packed it in.

Moving away from the town we were unsure as to what to do next. Money was getting extremely low and it didn't help with us having to eat in any small café that we could find. If this carried on, we would completely run out of funds before the end of the week.

Having one of his rare brainwaves Bob hit upon an idea; in a small outback town about thirty miles from our present position lived an aunt and uncle of his; we could go and pay them a visit. After telling them that we were on holiday they would put us up for a few days, giving us a chance to think about our next move. I didn't like the idea too much, but as I didn't have an alternative, I agreed to go along with it anyway.

After managing to hitch a ride in a car that was heading in the direction we arrived at the town and soon managed to find the house. Bob's relations seemed genuinely pleased to see him and after listening to the holiday story, they invited us both to stay at their place if we wanted to. After thanking them for their offer we were shown to a bedroom with the suggestion that perhaps we would like to have a shower, change our clothes and join them for dinner.

We had a very pleasant meal followed by an interesting conversation which involved such questions as, where were we planning to go? Did Bob's parents know where we were and how had Bob and I first met? Bob answered most of the questions truthfully whilst deviating slightly from the truth when the occasion arose. All in all, it seemed like a successful evening, and when it was time for bed, we both congratulated ourselves on a job well done! We had a good night's sleep for the first time in days, and the following morning, we were both full of life and bouncing around like two-year-olds.

During the day we ran a few errands for the aunt and generally, in between meals, made ourselves useful. In the early evening, the uncle returned from work and we all sat down to dinner before Bob asked them if they would mind if, after the meal, the two of us went for a walk and explored the town. After telling us that there was not much to see, they willingly agreed, and so we both went to see what the town had to offer.

It was nothing but a sleepy Australian outback village that catered for the surrounding sheep stations. It had one central street with a small assortment of shops, two pubs, and little else. After walking the full length of the street, we turned around and, whilst chatting to each other, started to return toward the house and call it a night. Suddenly, out of the corner of my eye, I sensed, rather than saw, a hand sweep down and smack Bob across the side of his head. Suspecting that, for no reason we were about to be attacked by the locals I turned around and squared up to the two massive-looking guys that were standing behind us. I was just about to throw a punch at one of the two attackers when Bob spoke up and I let my arms fall to my sides.

"It's my father!" he said.

Chapter Twenty-Eight

The four of us walked back to the house with the father showing and letting it be known that he wasn't exactly pleased with his son. We learned that Bob's uncle had phoned the father the night before, and the two had between them, arranged to let us remain there whilst the father and his friend, taking it in turns to drive, travelled by car overnight from Newcastle to the town where Bob and I were staying.

Under instructions from his old man both Bob and I packed our bags and after apologising to the aunt and uncle for the lie and thanking them for their hospitality, we both got into the backseat of a car and with his father driving and the friend in the front passenger seat. With Bob and I sitting on the back seat we started on the long drive to Newcastle, New South Wales.

We had been driving for hours with no one speaking when I felt Bob quietly tap my leg. Glancing down, I could just make out in the darkness that he was trying to pass me something and realised that it was all the money that we had left between us. I took it from him and quickly slipped it into my trousers' pocket. We travelled on and on in the car with no conversation apart from the odd words between the father and his friend. Sometime later Bob's father stopped the car in the middle of nowhere and unceremoniously told me that this was where his son and I would be parting company. I got out of the car and without so much as a goodbye the three drove off, leaving me standing there in complete silence alongside the dirt road whilst watching the red taillights disappear into the distance.

It was pitch black, and I could hardly see a hand in front of me. Remembering that there was grass scrubland running alongside the dirt, I did the only thing that it was possible to do, I lay down on the grass and tried to sleep until the dawn broke.

By the time, the first glimmer of light appeared over the horizon I was wide awake and sitting on my suitcase. What was I supposed to do now I wondered?

I checked my pockets and found the few quid that Bob had given me earlier. Well, that was a start at least, I wasn't completely broke, not that a few quid would go far.

The sun started to rise in the sky and with it the heat seemed to encapsulate the road and the area surrounding it. I was still sitting on my suitcase as a few early morning vehicles started driving past on their way to make morning deliveries. It was whilst watching these trucks that I made my mind up that I would try to thumb a lift to Newcastle, the only place that I knew for sure to be at the end of the road I was on. After I arrived there I could see if I could locate Bob. I didn't make any further plans at that time, although I knew that I was in dire straits with no money, no job, nowhere to live and again, seemingly no friends. I waited a while before spotting the now-familiar plume of dust approaching in the distance that informed me of a fast-approaching vehicle and steeled myself to start hitchhiking; luckily for me the car stopped and asked where I was heading.

Newcastle really surprised me; I was expecting a small town but as the driver, who had given me the lift, stopped to set me down I could see that it was an exceptionally large city. Considering that I didn't know Bob's home address or even the area where his house was located the situation presented me with an enormous task and little chance of success. However, now was not the time to give up but more of a chance to think positively and see if I could solve the challenge that lay before me! After all, since my arrival in Australia, I had managed to overcome many other challenges.

My first job was to try and find, however temporary, some form of accommodation. This would be no easy task with the small amount of money I had in my pocket. I wandered the wide, busy streets, looking for somewhere that looked cheap to stay before realising that I was very hungry and settled for a small café where I ordered myself the cheapest sandwich on the menu. Eating it very slowly I made it last for quite some time. After poking my finger at the crumbs left on the plate and then popping my finger into my mouth so as not to waste anything, I paid the bill and asked the cashier if she knew of anywhere to get a cheap room for the night? She didn't have much of an idea—of anything. In fact, it was quite difficult to get any words of English or any other language for that matter, out of her. On leaving the café that I had decided to name 'the scruffy dump' I continued with my footslogging around the town. I hadn't gone very far when I came across an old building with a dilapidated sign that informed me that it was 'The Salvation Army Hotel'. It must be cheap, I informed myself and marched into the lobby like a good Salvation Army Officer would be expected to do whilst ready to break into a rousing chorus of 'Onward Christian Soldiers'.

It may have been a Christian haven, but it didn't seem to be too inexpensive to me however, I managed to wrangle a room from the manager after emphatically stating that I would pay the room rate in the next few days before checking out. I dragged my suitcase up a flight of stairs and entered my new five-star accommodation.

The room had a close relationship with the railway hostel in which I had lived in Melbourne. However, as a now-practising Christian, I decided that it would be a suitable place from which to fight my own personal war and in going about my business trying to find Bob.

After entering the room my first act was to sit on the bed and take stock of my position. Here I was, singing Christian hymns in a cheap hostel, spending money, of which I didn't have, in a city that I didn't know and in a country that I didn't like. It sounded like the perfect storm to me. Checking my pockets, I found that my entire fortune added up to about an Australian pound. That was hardly enough to buy a cheap meal. Forgetting dinner for the night I laid on the bed and fell into a restless sleep.

The following morning, I awoke and after taking a shower, I walked the streets looking for a telephone booth. My luck was in; I found one, and to my delight it contained a telephone directory. I left the phone-box and changed my one-pound note into coins at a local shop before returning to the booth and quickly looking up Bob's family name. There were hundreds of them listed; either it was an extremely popular name or his family bred like rabbits!

Putting money into the coin box I started phoning around and asking to speak to Bob but, much to my disappointment, I kept getting the same answer. There was no Bob living at that address. With the money quickly disappearing into the phone's money box it wasn't long before I was forced to give up making the calls.

Now what could I do? Nothing! I didn't have enough money to keep calling and it would have been impossible to walk around each area of a large town looking for him. Even if I found him, it was impossible to tell if he could or would be able to help me, he may have even been placed in chains by his parents!

I slowly walked back to my room, a room that was racking up more debt by the minute. Sitting on the bed I felt more and more depressed and had absolutely no idea of how to solve my problem. I had no one who I could turn to for help. I couldn't stay in this hotel much longer without being asked to pay the bill and had no way of getting a job to make any money without first finding somewhere to live; finally, lady luck had caught up with me!

The more I thought the more I realised that there simply wasn't an answer to my predicament. No one else was to blame, I had brought the whole thing on myself. If I hadn't listened to other people, I could have been still working in Melbourne or even Sydney and had money in my pocket and a place to stay. I had tried, at least I felt I had, but there was no way I could carry on like this. Feeling as if I had no other options left to me, I went out of the room and made my way to a local chemist shop. I spent the last of my money making a purchase before I again returned to the room. Strangely, I felt happier now, almost peaceful; sure, I wouldn't be able to go back to the UK, but it wouldn't matter very much either. All my problems would be ended in one foul swoop with nothing more to worry about!

I kept reminding myself that I really had no choice as I started to crush the purchase I had made earlier into a powder. I added water to the granules and stirred it into a thick creamy-looking mess; just a little more water and it would be ready to swallow. Starting to cry to myself at the thought of what I was about to do I put the extra water into the glass. I was about to drink the stuff when I had one final thought; probably talking to myself I said, "God, if you really do exist, maybe we'll be meeting up soon and then we can compare notes." I could see my gravestone and the epitaph written on it would be, 'Here lays Brian Robson, a victim of Australia!'

I forced as much of the stuff as I could down my throat before feeling that I was going to vomit. Trying to relax and feeling very unwell, I lay down on the bed and waited to pass into the next world!

Chapter Twenty-Nine

Without having any real feeling of my body, I could hear bells ringing in my ears. The noise could best be described as very loud and completely out of both timing and tune; it was more a colophony of sound. I opened my eyes and everything around me was a blur; nothing was in focus and the more I tried to correct my sight, the worse the colophony in my ears became. It wasn't long before the thoughts of what I had done began returning to me.

The completely out of focus and blurred picture that was all I could see was bathed in a bright light, and with the sound of the bells still ringing, I guessed that I must be in heaven. Suddenly—and completely in focus—a woman's face appeared barely a few inches from my nose. In an Australian accent she asked me how I felt and, although I didn't answer her, I felt appalled at the thought that even here they had Australian angels! I began to imagine that each country must have its own heaven, so now I was stuck with Australians for eternity. The thought made me quickly close my eyes again!

As my thoughts started to clear for the second time, I slowly opened my eyes and began to realise that the place that I had thought of as being heaven was in fact, a hospital! Thank God that the angels I thought I had seen were not angels at all but Australian nurses.

I had no recollection of how I had ended up in a hospital or how long I had been here. The last thing I could remember before waking up a few moments ago was crushing those tablets into powder and drinking the horrid mess. Various people started to make visits to my bedside and most poked me around a little before I slowly started to make a bit of a recovery and gather my senses together. The ringing sound in my ears persisted and as much as I shook my head refused to go away. Except for feeling depressed, it was perhaps three days before my body was feeling more its normal self.

One day during his usual visit, the doctor told me that I would be transferred to another hospital, and perhaps there they would be able to help me with the depression. To me, nothing was that important anymore so I just nodded my head and waited for the transfer to take place. Sure enough, later that day they placed me in the back of an ambulance, and we drove to the new hospital.

Upon arriving, I was shown into an office where two doctors were sitting behind desks. They seemed quite cheerful and quite the opposite to the way I felt as, I had no interest in anything and couldn't even be bothered by saying hello. As they were chatting to me—and being ignored—one of them started to smoke a cigarette, and that managed to get my attention. "Can I have one of those?" I asked, nodding at his cigarettes.

"Sure, you can!" He passed me the packet and I took one out. "How are you feeling now?"

"I'm okay, but my stomach feels as if it wants to be sick, and I have bells ringing in my ears."

"That's pretty normal with aspirin poisoning; don't worry, it'll pass given time."

"Do I look worried?" I muttered back at him.

That was the end of my interest in the conversation; I didn't want to talk to anyone and had very little intention of listening to them however, I did catch the part where they said that I would be staying there for a while and we'll see what happens next.

What happens next? Who cares what happens next; why won't people just leave me alone—completely alone! That would be better for them and for me. It was no good my telling them my thoughts as they, like all the rest, would take no notice of anything that I say.

It was a rather small hospital with only two wards, one for male and one for female patients with about fifteen beds in each. There was a television lounge next to a dining room and attached to the main building was a small room with a few indoor games. The doctors each had an office in a corridor opposite the nurse's room, and next to that, a small room for dispensing medicine. Everything seemed very new and rather upbeat for a hospital with all the staff, both doctors and nurses, being over-friendly and amazingly even trying to be helpful.

I was taken to a bed in the male ward and after lying down, I soon fell asleep. Waking up a few hours later I went for a walk around the place and after poking my nose in here and there, I bumped into one of the nurses. She asked me the perfunctory question of how I was feeling, and after sarcastically informing her that I was fine and on top of the world, she asked if I wanted something to eat. I ended up sitting with her in the nurse's room, eating part of a meal and starting to ask a few questions.

I discovered that the place was an assessment centre where doctors decided if you were slightly insane or completely around the bend. After they had assessed you, they would decide on how best to help, and if that meant receiving some sort of physiocratic treatment or other medical help they would offer it. I couldn't wait for them to decide if I would be going to a small mental hospital or just released into the big one known as Australia! That night I lay awake wondering exactly how I had managed to get myself into such a mess and wondering what was happening back in Wales, Wales UK that was!

The next morning, I had breakfast in the dining room with the other inmates and kept looking to see if anyone was pulling funny faces or which ones didn't look quite normal. I couldn't spot anyone and thought that they must all be covering it up quite well. I was inclined to pull a few faces myself to see what reaction I would get but decided against it as I might set the whole place off.

With breakfast over and wondering if I should be walking around looking a bit doolally it came as quite a relief when a nurse came up and told me that the doctor wanted to see me. I went to the office and after knocking on the door was told to come in. Following instructions, I did as I was told and sat down on a chair with a lady doctor sitting behind the desk in front of me.

She asked me how I was feeling and about the ringing in my ears. It was only when she mentioned the ringing that I realised that it had stopped and that I was now back to my normal self and able to leave this mental hospital. I told her my thoughts and she just smiled at me; so, for good luck, I added, "Oh, and by the way, I'm not mad!"

"Who said that you were?" she asked me.

"No one, I just want to clarify the point."

"So, why don't you tell me how you ended up here?"

"I came in an ambulance," I answered.

"I mean the reason you ended up here?"

"Well, why didn't you ask that?"

"Maybe I meant to," she said with a smile, "are you going to tell me?"

"I suppose so."

"Well, go on then; just take your time."

"It's all about Australia," I began, "and a long story!"

"Tell me, I've got plenty of time," so, I did. I told her the entire sordid truth!

I finished my tale of woe and ended up with, "So you see, just a passport and enough money to pay my fare out of here, and I'll be gone, completely out of your way!" She smiled whilst appearing to think for a few minutes before finally speaking.

"Have you ever heard of repatriation?" she asked me. I nodded my head before she added, "Well, perhaps we should recommend that they repatriate you!"

"Would they?" I asked, sounding much more interested in the conversation.

"Yes, I think so, but it will take a while to arrange; look, if you promise me that you'll relax a bit more, and if you feel that you have a problem, you'll seek help, then we'll start the process of moving."

"Seek help from where?" I half-smiled.

"Here might be a good start?"

"If I agree with that, does it mean that I can leave here now?"

Grinning, she said, "You can leave here anytime you want to, but that's not a good idea! Let us give it a few more days before we talk of leaving; if that's okay with you?"

I nodded in agreement, suddenly realising that I was in love with her. I had finally found someone who understood that I just wanted to go home.

Leaving the doctor's office, I felt much happier than before I went in, and heading straight to the nurse's room, I informed all that were present that the doctor told me I was going to be repatriated. They all seemed happy for me and one said that as they were all helping me, perhaps I could help them out a bit.

"Help you how?" I asked.

"There are many ways to help, for example, we have a young girl in the ladies ward who's quite depressed and she needs someone to maybe play table tennis with. If you played with her, you might be able to cheer her up a bit?"

I didn't know about 'cheering her up' but anyway I agreed and so, Jenny and I played table tennis a few hours each day over the next few days. We were both useless at it, but we managed to entertain each other. During the breaks in between games, we just sat and talked, and it was during one of these chats that I discovered that she was in the place for the same reason as I had ended up there.

I told her that it was a stupid thing to do, and she told me that I was not the one to talk as we had done the same thing! We both laughed after I admitted that she may well be right but that I had had a good reason. I told her all about the UK and how I had to get back there as Australia had been a big mistake. She told

153

me about the family problems she had which had caused her to do the same thing. We made a pact between us that neither would try to do it again no matter what the circumstances.

One night, we were both watching some boring TV programme when for some reason the Welsh song *Suo Gân* started to play. I felt a bit weepy, and leaving the room, I went through the veranda door, and sat there looking up at a full moon.

Jenny came out and without speaking just sat alongside me. "Are you okay?" she asked.

"Yeah, I'm just feeling homesick, the music reminded me of Wales and you see that moon?" She looked up at the sky. "That's the same moon as people will be able to see back in the UK."

"I suppose that it must be," she said, giggling, "we've only got the one!"

"I know that. I'm just saying…"

"Saying what?" She mocked.

"Saying…" I changed track, "…do you want a game of table tennis?"

We both quickly stood up and raced each other to the game's room.

Chapter Thirty

Jenny was finally discharged from the hospital and sent home where, apparently; all her problems had been sorted out. I missed her quite a lot, and it must have shown on my face as the nurses seemed to find me more and more things to do to keep me busy. Apart from running around helping them, watching television and seeing the doctor once a day, I in truth, had little to do.

One day whilst visiting the doctor, she informed me that I was fine, and she could see no problem in her discharging me. She then told me that the next day the administration office would give me an address in Newcastle to go to and have a look at some accommodation that had been arranged for me. If I didn't like it, there was no reason to stay in the place, as other accommodation was available should I decide that I'd like to look at it. At that time, it crossed my mind that had the Victorian Railways done something like that, then, perhaps, none of this would have happened and I would still have been working for them!

I was given directions on how to get to the place that I could rent and given some money to pay for the bus fare that I would have to catch in order to get there. One of the nurses asked me if, whilst I was going on my travels, I could help by paying a bill for her. I agreed and she gave me the money to pay it and some extra to buy myself a packet of cigarettes. I told her that she didn't need to give me extra money as it would not be a problem in paying the bill for her. However, she insisted, so I walked to the shop, paid her bill, bought myself a packet of cigarettes and then caught a bus to the nearby suburb where the accommodation was located.

The accommodation was in a house owned by an Italian lady who also lived there and cooked the meals for the five lodgers who were in residence. I met with her and she showed me around a quite well-kept property; we then sat at the dining table and had a chat. I didn't know if she knew anything about my reasons for needing a room, and so I decided not to say anything and keep my mouth shut unless she mentioned it first.

If I decided to move in, I would be sharing a room with one other person and would have two meals per day, breakfast in the morning and dinner in the evening. I would not need to pay rent until after I had managed to find a job and been paid my first week's wage, as apparently, someone else would pay it. I hadn't mentioned the hospital but, I thought it best not to ask who would pay, but it must be them as I didn't know anyone else who would offer to pay my rent. She ended by telling me that there were no restrictions on coming and going but that I could not bring friends back, as I didn't have any at the time, it didn't seem to matter too much.

After she had finished telling me the rules, she called some of the lads who lived there, and we all sat together and had a general chat. They told me that as far as lodgings went the place was good and that I could do a lot worse in other places. Taking in all they said and beginning to agree with them, I told the landlady that I would move in the next day, and with that, everything was settled.

I went straight back to the hospital and told them what had happened and of my future plans and they seemed quite pleased with the arrangements, even telling me that I would be given a small sum of money the next day to help me get organised.

With my promise that should I feel the need to I would go back and visit them, I moved into my new accommodation. I met up with the lads again and soon found out that they were all employed by B.H.P, located a short bus ride from the house in which we were all living.

B.H.P were the initials of 'Broken Hill Proprietaries', one of Australia's largest steel companies, and the following day I was in their personnel office applying for a job. Apparently, the State of New South Wales wasn't as finickity with its labour laws as the State of Victoria. Although my age hadn't changed, I was offered a job working on the nightshift. I found this quite funny; I was too young to work shifts in one state, but much sought after in another. Where else but Australia would you find such an assortment of mixed-up and ridiculous rules?

Soon after my interview I started work and quickly got used to working nights. We even had time during the night shift to take a one-hour nap which was usually arranged to take place just after the early morning meal break. Another advantage of working at night was that unlike the daytime, the night air was quite cool and there was no sun to bother you, a distinct advantage when working and compared to the heat of the average Australian day. Another advantage of working those hours was that I had plenty of time to sleep in the day and then after lunch to get into all sorts of minor trouble with two of the other lads who were working the same shift and living at the same address. One of them had an old motorcycle, and it wasn't long before he and I started travelling back and forth to the steelworks together on the battered old bike. His riding wasn't exactly brilliant, and a few times we nearly came off the thing; it was, however, all part of the fun! Although I had never ridden a motorcycle before I was soon practising how to ride it and even learnt how to do wheelies, much to the annoyance of other people living in the street.

I suppose that I had been working at B.H.P for nearly a month when one of the two lads I was living with had a small accident at work. A small slither of metal from a grinder had flashed up and lodged in his eye. The metal which was probably no bigger than a speck of dust was more irritating than harmful but meant that his eye would not stop watering. After work the next day and following a quick sleep, he wanted to go to the local hospital to let them have a look at it and so, I and the other lad went with him, more to keep him company than anything else. We travelled on a local bus and after arriving at the hospital were only waiting a short time before the doctor called him into the surgery. Within ten minutes he was back in the waiting room with his medical problem solved.

All three of us left the hospital and made it as far as the nearest milk bar. Succumbing to thirst, we stopped, sat down and ordered milkshakes. Merrily chatting and drinking away one of the lads told us about an idea he had had. It boiled down to the fact that we were all paying rent to live in our accommodation and the landlady was making a profit from our combined payments. Well, suppose we all clubbed together and found a house that was for rent? We would have more room to share and save money on the deal! The idea sounded quite good, but where would we find a house? That wasn't a problem, he informed us, as he already knew of a property that was available. The total rent of the house being fifty per cent of the money that the three of us were presently paying. Food would not be a problem as we could all eat at work or in a local café. The idea sounded quite good to both of us and we agreed that the next day we would go and have a look at the property before making up our minds. Finishing the drinks, we then left the milk bar. Things seemed to be looking up for me, I had two new friends, a job and a doctor who was helping me get repatriated back to the United Kingdom; what more could I wish for?

Laughing and cracking jokes, we started to walk back to the bus stop intending to catch a bus back home when, about thirty yards from reaching the stop I noticed a car that was parked in front of us and on our side of the road. Although I vaguely noticed it, I didn't pay it too much attention but, as we drew level with the front passenger window a man wound down the window and called out my name. All three of us stopped and I confirmed to the man that it was indeed my name that he had called out. At first, I was very confused that anyone in Newcastle would know me, but it slowly dawned on me that the men must be from the hospital and I asked that question. Nodding his head, he confirmed that my thoughts were correct and suggested that I jump in the back of the car for a few moments as he had something personal to tell me.

Telling my friends that I would only be a few minutes, I followed his suggestion and jumped into the backseat. Both men in the car turned around and told me that what they had to say was private that I should pull the door closed; I duly obliged and closed it. It was only then that one of the men informed me that what they really wanted to talk to me about was a matter of a few bounced cheques!

Chapter Thirty-One

They were quite a friendly pair who drove me back to my lodgings to collect my property and even drove me over to B.H.P to collect the money that I was owed for working. I was so impressed with them that I did think of offering them a tip or at least some money to cover a taxi fare, but after lulling the idea over, I concluded that they were already being paid for supplying the service.

During our drive around Newcastle, it was explained to me that they were police officers and that the guy sitting in the front passenger seat and I would be travelling up to Brisbane, where I was to attend court. That was only after I had been charged with being Australia's most wanted criminal at the main Newcastle police station! I started to wonder if we would be hitchhiking back up to Brisbane but was pleased to learn that we would be flying. It felt a little like a holiday atmosphere as I wondered if they had booked a hotel for me to stay at as well.

Once we had arrived at the local police station, the guy that was taking me back to Brisbane signed some forms and arranged for a car to take us to the airport. It was certainly nice of him and much nicer than going by bus! He explained to me that if I behaved myself, we could travel together as father and son and that we wouldn't need handcuffs or even a leg chain and iron ball. The idea sounded good to me, and so I agreed with his proposal. He carried my suitcase and at the airport he even checked it in with the airline for me. I did consider offering to buy the tickets for both of us but, by that stage, I had no idea what I had done with my cheque book!

The flight was quite pleasant and before arriving at our destination, we had a glass of orange juice each.

After disembarking from the aircraft, I was quite disappointed to find a police van waiting for me and felt even unhappier when I discovered that I was expected to sit in the back of it. At the very least, a car would have been more appropriate for a prisoner of my stature! Sitting for the first time behind bars, all be it in a police van, I decided that from now on and until my escape, I would class myself as a prisoner of war, having been taken prisoner by the nearest thing to the Japanese army, the Australians.

Who'd have thought it? They were supposed to have been on our side during the war! If Mr Churchill had known how two-faced they were, he wouldn't have been so polite towards them! I could see it in the UK newspapers now, 'Australians take British prisoner of war!' Maybe the Second World War had ended seventeen years earlier, but it was obvious that the Australians had not heard the news as of yet!

We drove the short distance from the airport to the police station where I was placed in a cell right opposite the office of the enemy. I could see right in and watched them making the poisoned tea that they would then try and persuade people to drink. They couldn't catch me out as I had watched too many black and white war films to fall for that old trick.) Be nice to them and pretend that you were on their side then, after accepting the tea, wait for them to walk away and tip the tea down the loo. They had met their match in wartime espionage.

After surviving the night without being poisoned, I was taken upstairs to a place that they had cleverly disguised as a court of law and after completely ignoring the military tribunal that took place, I was brought back downstairs again. Sixty days seemed to be the general verdict that I, whilst pretending to ignore what was going on, had listened to. That was their plan. Sixty days on bread and water; it didn't alter my determination, once the war had ended, I'd get them on war crimes!

And so, I was taken to the central jail in Brisbane where I would be held captive for the next two months. After having a shower, I was given a Japanese-style uniform and a pair of long pants before being taken to see the camp commander, who was masquerading as the Governor of the jail. Asking me if I knew why I was in the place I quickly informed him that I was a prisoner of war and that after the British invasion of Australia, I would be set free. I think that he thought that I was slightly mad, but it was one thing thinking and quite another knowing the truth.

The camp commander and his minions had a quick discussion before telling me that I would be put to work with the team who dealt with the electrical repairs of the camp, then they marched me off with the music of 'Colonel Bogey' resounding in my ears! I was given some food and locked away for the night, giving me time to reflect on my surroundings and make plans for my next action.

The following day, at some God-forsaken hour, I was woken up and after joining the other members of the junior division, were all paraded into what would later become known as the exercise yard. This gave me some time to get an eye for the lay of the land or at least see where I was!

The concentration camp was split into two halves each surrounded by a high wall. On one side were kept the junior prisoners and about one hundred older guys who had been accused of various white-collar crimes. The compound consisted of two buildings for accommodating the prisoners: a reception area, complete with showers for new arrivals, a kitchen and two yards, one for the white-collar type and one for us. During the day and above each of the yards, there was a geek with a rifle looking down. In the centre of all these buildings was a courtyard, and to get anywhere, everyone had to pass through one gate or another to get into this yard before then heading towards one's destination.

In the accommodation building, the ground floor was reserved for the junior division and the upper two floors for the older guys. The sleeping area was supposed to be a single room, each with its own locked door, but if the place got too busy with new arrivals the junior division got shoved in together with three people in a room to make space for the newcomers. With only one bed in each room the other two occupants had to make do with mattresses on the floor which meant that every night, there was a big scramble to see who was first to get the bed.

The other side of the jail had the same layout but was much bigger and included workshops, bakery and a small shed where the people repairing the prison camps electrical faults worked. To get from one side of the place to the other there was quite a long underground tunnel with a metal gate on each end, and although no one was sure, it was believed that above-ground, a road ran between the two places. It was especially important to make plans of the place as no one was sure when they would try and make a break for it and it was not possible to buy maps.

For me, it was the first time that I had met real Australians. They all seemed a much friendlier bunch than the imposters outside the place.

The first morning I was to go to work I was collected by a guard from the exercise yard and taken through the underground tunnel to the second jail before being handed over to a guy in the electrical repair hut. He seemed like a friendly chap but was on the side of the enemy. We spoke to each other politely and he introduced me to the others who also worked there.

In all, there was the boss who was an electrician, an older guy who lived on our side of the camp and was also a qualified electrician and, including me, three others from the junior brigade who didn't know much about anything but were used for changing light bulbs when the occasion arose.

After I had been introduced to everyone their first question was what was I doing there and I, deciding to start where I intended to finish, explained that I was a prisoner of war and would be released after the British army invaded Australia!

Mike, who was also a member of the junior division and who incidentally rented the room next to mine back in the prisoner of war camp must have been trying to read a book sometime earlier, as he informed me that I couldn't be a prisoner of war as it had already ended!

"You're joking, right?" he asked me.

"Nope, I'm a prisoner of war until my release from this internment camp."

Giggling, he asked what else I was in there for so, I explained that someone had mentioned a few dud cheques, but as I didn't recognise any law not passed by the British government, they could stick that and I was only obliged to give my name, rank and number.

"Do you have a number?"

"Not yet, I'm working on it," I replied.

Mike and I got on famously and it was only a matter of a few days before he and most of the others in the junior division had joined the prisoner of war society. We all agreed with whatever our guards told us, but we took no notice of them whatsoever and whenever possible did the complete opposite to what was asked of us.

Most of our days was spent changing light bulbs and most of the evening and nights sitting alone in our rooms which was fine but boring. What was needed was some sort of code where we could communicate with each other 24/7 and without the enemy having any idea what we were talking about. I solved that problem by inventing a simple but brilliant code system. I converted the alphabet from letters into twenty-six numbers which we could use. For example, the letter 'A' became one, 'B' two and on up to twenty-six. These numbers we could tap out on the wall separating each room and the guy in the next room would do the same and so on right down the row of rooms. Once written down on a piece of paper, the number of taps would be matched to its corresponding letter of the alphabet and formed into a word or sentence. With the plan explained to each prisoner of war we were finally ready to put it into action.

At about six every evening, one of the guards entered the building and would walk down the length of the wing checking all the doors. Putting our plan into action, the prisoner in the last room would know that he was coming without even having to look out of his room. A message was prepared 'the guard is coming' and converted into numbers for the tapping process. Sure enough, at six on the dot, the guard entered the building and the tapping on the wall began. The guard walked the length of the building before turning around and walking back to the main door where he left the wing. Twenty minutes after he had gone our tapped message finally reached the last room and the prisoner of war, who was held captive in there, received the message 'the guard is coming!' Obviously, this flaw in the system could not be allowed to continue, and so collectively we spent weeks trying to improve our plan before finally giving up and binning the idea.

One messaging system that worked involved sending messages to another concentration camp located about twenty miles away from ours. This camp was cleverly disguised as a jail farm and as the Queensland government was too mean to employ two electricians—one for each camp—they sent our boss there once or twice a week. To help him fix the electrical problems the older guy who worked with us and me were put in the back of a pickup and driven to the farm where I used to pass messages between the prisoners from our concentration camp to the others and vice versa. We'd also have lunch there which was of much better quality than back in our place, so I didn't mind and looked forward to going!

Chapter Thirty-Two

Apparently, it was a busy period at the Brisbane nick, and they were short of space. If only they would have asked us, we would all have helped them out by leaving, but then they were not known for their common sense! Mike, I and another lad were put in the same room to make space for the new prisoners. The war must have been going very badly with the arrival of the new detainees; however, we were doing our bit to make them feel at home.

One night, all three of us were joking around when the idea of escape came to mind. Although I only had about twenty-five days left to do and the other kid just a little bit more, Mike assured us that as prisoners of war, it was our bound duty to make at least one attempt at escaping.

He had been trying to read a book and that was always a dangerous time with him as he only managed to understand about every third word and so he sometimes got the gist of the book wrong. Anyway, according to his book, if you tied some material such as cotton in a long rope, soaked it in water and then tied both ends together and twisted the whole thing as it started to dry out, it would shrink. If it were tied to say, the window bars and the bottom corner of the door in the cell, the pressure would be so great that the door would be forced open!

He was positive that if we tried it, it would work and then all three of us would be free. We reminded him that if we managed to open the door and get out of the room it would put us in the hallway of the building, and what would we do then? The hallway was also covered with iron bars at both ends. So, if we managed to get into the hallway and turned either left or right, our escape path would be blocked by a massive array of these bars which, as we agreed with Mike, had a door located in them. Of course, these doors were also made of metal bars and would be locked from the outside.

This was a mere hiccup according to him, the important thing being to get out of the room, and all other details could be worked out after this had been achieved. We spent the rest of the night making plans for the great escape, but as the door was made up of a sheet of solid iron, we had our doubts that a couple of cotton sheets would have the power to bend it! Another idea was raised by Mike; if one of the door hinges was broken, it would be much easier to complete the plan, but how would we break the hinge?

We could pinch a cold chisel from the electrical workshop then, by using that and hitting it with the heel of a shoe, we could keep banging away at the hinge until it broke, or until someone heard the noise that we would be making and reported it to the authorities.

All the major problems were dismissed, as it was accepted that we would get into the hallway surrounded by iron bars and break through them, then we need to get into a corridor with more iron bars, get over a twenty-foot wall, then climb a twenty-foot chain fence on the other side before finally scaling a twenty-foot brick wall and with all the guards hanging around and ignoring us! Both I and my other roommate were quite sure that the plan wouldn't work, but Mike was quite convinced that his book had got it right and even gave us an example involving the washing of a shirt which can shrink, 'right?' So, finally, we agreed to go ahead with him and do it.

The following day, we all went to work, and I spent most of the day sniffing through toolboxes looking for exactly the right cold chisel to do the job. Finding one that suited the situation, I secreted it on my person and smuggled it back into our room. The great escape was on!

As soon as darkness fell, we started banging the hinge, but the more we banged it, the more nothing happened. We were overjoyed at one stage when we missed hitting the hinge altogether but managed to hit the cement surrounding it and a little bit of the cement came flying out. That hole would soon be spotted by our guards, we told Mike, but he was quite sure that if we filled it up with soggy bread no one would notice it and the bread could be removed when we were finally ready for the escape to take place.

Giving up on the hinge idea, we focused our attention on the shrinking material part of our plan. We ripped the bedsheets into thick strips and soaked them in water then, after twisting the entire length, we joined the ends together to form a circle by tying them around the window bars and slipped the looped end under the corner of the door. We broke a leg off the table and pushed it through the twists in the sheet before twisting the table leg to tighten up the whole circle of the wet bedsheet even more. After completing our task, we all sat down to take a rest and watch our idea come to fruition.

It was like watching wet paint dry, nothing happened! After a few hours of staring at it and with all that work we had ended up with something that resembled a washing line full of twisted up sheets that had been blown by the wind and, what's more, the door hadn't budged an inch! All we were left with was a three-legged table and no sheets to sleep on for the night.

The night passed slowly and from time to time we debated what had gone wrong with our wonderful idea. What was at fault, was it the sheet, the door or Mike's misreading of the book? All we were left with was a room that looked as though a bomb had gone off in it and an escape plan that for some mysterious reason we had had to cancel. One thing that urgently needed to be taken care of was the state of the room as nobody would believe that a hurricane had whipped through the place overnight! Early the next morning, I spoke to the landing orderly, who was a friend of mine and responsible for all the property used in the rooms. I explained that the night before, we'd had an accident, and he agreed to give us a new four-legged table and sheets whilst promising not to tell the guards.

Whilst he was sorting out the new stuff, he commented on the noise that had kept most of the wing awake during the night.

"It sounded like someone was trying to escape." He laughed. Laughing with him, I commented,

"No one in their right mind would try that, would they?"

Chapter Thirty-Three

With the idea of escape gone from our minds, things got back pretty much to normal until one day, when we were all together in our little electrician's hut, the boss man sounding half apologetic, told me that he was not allowed to take me to the farm anymore.

"…And why not?" I snapped at him, thinking that it might have something to do with the many electrical cables that I had deliberately damaged every time I went there.

"Because apparently, they're going to deport you, and you might prove to be an escape risk!"

"Deport me, escape risk," I repeated very slowly before breaking into a big smile as it sank in. "Are they mad? Why didn't they tell me before? If they're going to deport me, I'd do anything they want me to." I did a little song and dance before adding, "Anything!"

A few days after being told of my pending deportation, we were all back in our little electricity shed. It was first thing in the morning, and we were waiting for one of the paid goons to bring the daily worksheet. This was an especially important document as it would inform the boss man, and eventually us, of what light bulbs would need to be changed that day. The number of bulbs was the most important part of our workday as the three members of our junior division, who were all smokers, would put one rolled-up cigarette into a pot and before the document arrived would guess the number of changes needed. The one who made the closest guess would keep the whole pot of three cigarettes. Without this competition the daily excitement of changing the light bulbs would have ceased to exist.

Across the street from our electrical shed and a little to the right was the start of a building that housed the jail's workshops and about half an hour after we had started work, a great flux of people, walking single file and like a long snake would wind their way into the buildings to begin their days toil on one of the many sewing machines that were lined up in there.

During the night and for a reason known only to the owners of the concentration camp, a lonely goon with a pistol would be on patrol outside these buildings. Looking very smart in his uniform, he would spend a boring night talking to himself, with only his gun for company. As we, members of the electrical shed, were the first to arrive in the mornings, the boss man, who was always with us would shout a message to the goon with the gun who would then walk further away from us and we would enter our shed being safely protected in case the goon decided to use us for target practice. I suppose the idea was to keep us away from the gun he had on his hip because if people like Mike managed to get their hands on it, they would think that all their birthdays had come at once!

Well, this morning, we turned up as normal and went into our shed. The goon with the gun was in his usual place and we shouted our normal, if perhaps slightly two-faced, good morning to him. What we didn't know was that he was a smoker and had turned up for work the night before without any matches. He had spent the whole night desperate for a smoke and with no way of getting a light for his cigarette! The first we knew of all this was while we were hanging around the shed waiting for the daily lottery to arrive, he came in and asked if anyone had a light? Mike, who was the furthest away and in an amazing display of generosity, pulled out a match and offered it to the goon who walked between us, gun and all, and quickly lit his cigarette! He failed to notice that all of us were standing around with our mouths open in utter shock! Our boss man eventually told him that perhaps it would be a good idea to get the gun and himself the hell out of the place! Anyone of us could have very easily removed the gun from his waist and held the whole place hostage. I would hate to think of what could have happened if the goon had done the same thing with any other group apart from the jokers of the jail!

The final days of my 'prisoner of war' times had come to an end. Tomorrow would be the last day of my mixing with real Australians before my being deported back to my own country. The war would be over, and I would never need to return to this island again. Around midday, I was taken to see the governor of the penal colony—he didn't like to work a lot and so stayed in bed most of the day. Today, in my honour, he had fallen out of bed, semi-drunk, to come and say goodbye.

"So, Brian, you're leaving us tomorrow, right?"

"Yep." I smiled back. "And about time too!"

"I hope that it hasn't been too hard for you?"

"Nope, as 'prisoner of war' camps go, I can recommend it and there are worse places," I smiled at him before adding, "I guess!"

"You'll need to sign this paper." He passed a sheet of typed A4 over to me.

I read it slowly and it said something about my acknowledging that my property had been returned and that apart from getting my suitcase back (with all its contents), I would receive the money that had been collected on my behalf from the BHP steel works in Newcastle. I nodded my head before asking him a question, "so where's my ticket?"

"What ticket?" He looked a little surprised.

"My ticket to London, or am I supposed to walk?"

"What are you talking about?" he asked, trying to conjure up a smile.

"I'm being deported back to a civilised country, and for that, I need a ticket, right?"

"Deported? No, you're being released from here, not deported!"

I hit the roof; they had lied to me yet again! Would it not be possible for at least one person on this God-forsaken island to at least tell the truth? All the arguments I put forward fell on deaf ears; I would be free to go from the jail!

"I don't want to go; I want to be deported!"

"Well, you're not going to be!"

"Then I'm not going anywhere; I'll stay right here!"

"You can't!"

"Who says I can't, you?"

"The law says that you can't!"

"The law's an ass! Are you telling me that your stupid laws kept me in here for sixty days when I was public enemy number one, and now, I don't even hold that exalted position? This is incredulous!" I was shouting by now. "Are you telling me that I'm not even a danger to the public? Well, I'm not going, and that's that!"

Refusing to sign the paper, I stormed out of the room with a suggestion to them of where they could stick it.

Chapter Thirty-Four

It was only about an hour later when I was very politely 'asked' if I would go and meet the governor again. This time we sat on opposite sides of his desk while he informed me, in what sounded like an almost apologetic tone, that they had forced people unwillingly into the place and stopped people from leaving, but to the best of his recollection they had never had anyone with the legal right to leave refusing to go!

We discussed the matter for over an hour before I realised that all the argument in the world was not going to get me anywhere and that tomorrow morning, like it or not, I would be thrown out. I felt at a new low, stuck in a country where I had no wish to be and subjected to the all-time insult by being thrown out of the local jail!

So, it came to pass, the next day I was homeless and without a chance of being deported. I wandered the streets for a while before drowning my sorrows with a milkshake and making plans for my future. One thing that was certain was that I would never trust any Australian official again, as far as I was concerned, they could all stay in the local nick where they belonged!

Alone and with just my suitcase for company I decided to return to Melbourne and see what sort of trouble I could cause for them there.

Two days later, after travelling by train, I arrived back in Melbourne where all my troubles had begun. The city hadn't changed much with the same dreary weather that I remembered from the last time I visited and immediately after my arrival I put myself to good use trying to find a place to stay.

I found a place owned by an Italian immigrant who was pocketing the rent whilst avoiding the need to pay tax on the money. The bedsitter was in an area of Melbourne called St Kilda. It was two rooms, a basic bedroom and the room next to it which had been converted into a small sitting area with a kitchen attached. It would do for the time being.

Now that I had secured somewhere to sleep, I needed to find a job to help pay for the rent.

A few days later whilst I was walking around Flinders Street Railway Station in central Melbourne I found, near the back of the building, a sign that informed everyone that workers were required. I went in and applied for a job in what transpired to be a paper mill. My application was immediately accepted, but the strange thing was that the workers were on strike and although I attended work every day, there was actually very little work to do; just sit around and wait until it was time to leave for home. Very boring, but why should I complain, I was getting paid for doing nothing!

Settling down to life in my bedsitter and going to work during the day made life chug on, but it didn't take long before I became completely bored. So bored, in fact, that one day after finishing my hanging around at work routine, I decided that I would go back and look at the hostel where I had started this epic adventure. The place was only a twenty-minute walk from where I was working so it wouldn't take much effort and would at least pass some time away. I soon arrived and the place looked the same as the first day I had arrived from the UK. I walked around as if I owned it and was quickly reminded that all my problems had started here. I couldn't wait to get out of the place and go home to St Kilda and as I was about to do so, I bumped into one of the residents. His name was Paul, and after saying hello, we had a brief conversation before he invited me into his room to meet a friend of his named John.

It turned out that they were both from Ireland and been friends since school days. As I had been doing in the past, they were both working for the railway. Neither of them liked living in Australia and so I was in good company. We chatted away for hours and got on so well that we agreed that I would forget my feelings about the hostel and come to visit them again the next day.

It didn't take long before we had all became good friends and used to do almost everything together. Sometimes, I would visit them and other times they would come over to St Kilda to visit me. They were extremely interested in many of the things that I had been up to in Australia, but the thing that mainly held us together was our mutual hate of the country in which we found ourselves living. That hate was generated by the feeling that we had all been lied to and let down by the people who had encouraged us to go there.

One evening, we were sitting at my kitchen table in St Kilda when Paul mentioned that there was some sort of British Exhibition being held in

171

Melbourne and that it might be a good idea if we all went and had a look at it; at least, it would give us something to do. So, the next day we all turned up at the Melbourne Showground…

Chapter Thirty-Five
Los Angeles, USA

I could feel the aircraft dropping slowly, and I knew that we were about to land somewhere. Tilting its wings and dropping even further, I reasoned that we couldn't be that far off a runway. I had absolutely no idea where we were, and it was difficult to even remember the number of stops we would have to make before we reached London. Was it eight or eighteen? I had no idea; my mind just wasn't functioning in the way it normally did. All that I understood was that I could feel nothing but the pain from the tip of my nose to the tip of my big toe.

The rush of speed as we hit the runway forced my body against the back wall of the crate and then let me go again as we slowed down. I went from a forced upright position back into the slouched position that I had adapted into during my journey. The aircraft stopped and taxied before coming to its final halt. After a few minutes, the doors of the 'planes hold was opened, and I could hear the by-now-familiar sound of muffled voices followed by the movement of freight. For some reason, this time it seemed different from all the other times and as the noises became clearer and clearer, I realised that the people unloading were speaking English. Suddenly, through the cracks, slits of light were entering the crate and the airport employees seemed to be completely emptying the hold of all its freight. My crate seemed to slide across the aircraft floor and was lifted into the air—quite abruptly I was outside the aircraft and could see the yellow lights of the airport. We had arrived; I was finally in London, and from the little I could see Heathrow Airport had never looked so good.

Along with all the other freight the crate I was in was placed on what seemed to be a luggage trolley that was attached to five or six other trolleys rather like a long snake. After taking five or six minutes to load it and with a jerk we started to move off, away from the plane and nearer to the airport lights. It wouldn't be long before I could break out of here, catch a bus and go home! Although experiencing periods of blackness and confusion I was trying to force myself into getting to grips with my surroundings and bringing my mind back into the real world. My mind seemed to react, but my body wouldn't move, and each attempt to move any part of it was met with more excruciating pain.

The chain of trolleys entered a large freight shed, and after it stopped, the crate I was in was taken off and placed on the ground. The trolley snake then moved off and left me in complete silence; I could almost hear my own heart beating.

The secret now was to get out of the crate unnoticed and that wasn't going to be easy. To do it, I would need to break open one side and then, not forgetting my suitcase, ease myself out. I'd need to find a gap in the fence surrounding the airport or find the passenger terminal and mix with the other passengers whilst looking for a way out. A final thought was that if all else fails, just find an official and tell him what I had done, even without a passport, they wouldn't throw me out, I'd lived here all my life, never held a passport and no one had ever told me to leave, so why would they start now?

It would be better to leave the crate and airport late at night, with hopefully, there being fewer people around, so I told myself to think, start thinking what I should be doing? Establishing the time would be a good idea, but although I had a wristwatch on there wasn't enough light in the crate to read the time on it. Then I remembered that less than two feet in front of my face was a small torch that we had hung on a nail when I was back in Melbourne. I tried to move my arm to reach for it but that was met with a searing pain and little or no movement. It seemed that all my muscles had somehow or other locked up. Nevertheless, I wasn't going to give in now not after coming all this way. Slowly, I forced my left arm to move inch by inch toward the torch. Between each attempt at movement, I paused, taking a deep breath and waited for the pain to subside before repeating the action again. It took what appeared to be an age to finally reach the torch. My fingers were as stiff as my arms, and as I tried to lift it, I accidentally turned the torch on whilst at the same time the beam of light lit the crate and the torch fell out of my grasp and with a loud bang ended up on the floor. Try as I might, I could not stretch my hand down far enough to reach it. I just sat there with a vague unsureness as to what to do next.

Five minutes had passed, and I had stopped the heavy breathing that I had adopted to control the pain as I tried to move; I was starting to calm down when I heard footsteps approaching and the sound of two people talking. To my horror,

I realised that they were speaking English with an American accent! This wasn't London; I was somewhere in the United States or Canada or New Zealand or somewhere!

What a disappointment! For the minute or so that it took to get used to the idea that this wasn't the UK, I felt deflated, almost defeated. After all that I had gone through I had completely failed on my mission. As the shock of not being in London started to sink in the clacking sound of the footsteps stopped. I heard and saw one of the men point in my direction and say to the other, "there's a light coming from that crate?" It was only then that I realised that the torch was still turned on just as they both walked toward me to take a closer look.

"What the hell could that be?"

"I don't know; have a look at the bill of loading and see what it says is inside the thing." They both looked at the paper attached to the crate.

"Computer parts for repair."

"Something must have turned itself on, is my guess."

One of the guys then spotted a small notch hole that, from the inside of the crate, was at eye level.

"There's a notch hole here, let me have a look and see if I can see inside!"

The guy bent down and put his eye to the small hole in the side of the crate. I couldn't move my neck and head and my eyes were just about level with the hole he was about to peer through. Focusing his vision to see in the darkness whilst looking inside. His eye made direct contact with mine before he jumped back a mile!

"There's a body in there!" he stammered. As for me trying to tell him I wasn't a body and I wasn't dead, it was impossible; my mouth would open, but no sound came out.

Both men were babbling to each other as they made a hasty retreat from the crate again leaving me alone. I was beginning to believe that my luck was in and that they wouldn't tell anybody when the warehouse became alive with the sound of voices and with many people heading in my direction. One of the men was speaking to the guy who had looked me right in the eye. "So, which crate is it?"

The guy pointed at my mode of transport before answering, "that one!" A second guy bent down and looked through the hole, then stood back in apparent shock.

"He's right Boss," he said, "there is a body in there!"

Chapter Thirty-Six

"I'm not a dead body, I'm alive!" I was yelling at them without any sound coming out of my mouth! Whilst I was trying to make contact, it appeared that they were having a meeting amongst themselves whilst trying to make a decision what should be done over the 'body' when, out of the blue, one of the guys bent down and again looked through the small hole in the side of the crate. He was trying to focus his vision when our eyes met; he blinked to refocus, and then, catching the movement of my eye, he almost jumped out of his skin!

Through lips that sounded almost drier and cracked worse than mine, he stammered, "It's not a body; whoever is in the crate is still alive!"

"Alive? Impossible!" Another guy who was looking over his shoulder said to him, "this crate has flown from...let's see," He glanced at the papers he was holding. "Sydney, Australia, and that's four and a half days away!"

"No, Sydney was a transit point; it started its journey in Melbourne, and that's over five days away!"

The hive of excitement grew and became even louder as they toyed with the idea of ripping the side of the crate off. The main argument against doing this seemed to arise from the fact that the crate was in transit and technically not in the United States, to open it would be breaking International Law.

Finally, one person who seemed to be in charge said, "Look, there's a human being in there, this is an emergency with no time to think of laws! Rip the side off, I'll take the responsibility!" Within seconds, his instruction was carried out and the side was ripped off. For the first time in five and a half days, I got a lungful of fresh air.

As soon as the crate was opened, two or three of the men helped lift me out and placed me on my back on the concrete floor. My legs however were still folded into my chest. They tried to straighten them out, but as fast as they lowered my legs, my body came up into a 45-degree angle. I had no feeling and no control over my body at all.

By now, there were maybe fifty to one hundred people either helping me or standing around and unsure of what to do. They consisted of many officials from such agencies as the FBI, The Airport Police, Pan American Airlines, The Los Angeles Police Force and many press and photographers. I was too far out of it to care or take much notice of any of them.

After being placed carefully on a stretcher, a group of people managed to straighten out my legs and I was eased into a waiting ambulance. With sirens blaring we raced through the city streets before arriving at a hospital which I was later to learn was the Los Angeles Central Receiving Hospital. I was examined by doctors who checked almost every part of my body including manipulating my arms, neck and legs, all of which I was still unable to move.

I still couldn't speak but my mind was ticking over, and I understood most of what was going on. Attempting to speak was sheer torture with my throat feeling as though I had two pieces of sandpaper lodged inside with one rubbing against the other. One thing that I couldn't understand was the large number of reporters, photographers and television crews who had amassed at the hospital in the short time it had taken us to travel from the airport in the ambulance. They seemed to be everywhere, but I was soon wheeled through the crowd and into the comparative quietness of a private examination room.

In the room, the reporters were replaced by what seemed to be a crowd of doctors, all interested to see what had arrived by crate. I was given oxygen from a mask placed over my mouth and nose and then again prodded and poked all over my body. My arms and legs were stretched out and manipulated into all angles. Although I felt pain in most positions, it stopped when the joints returned to their normal positions. After being given injections I was wheeled out of the room and after being undressed placed in a large tub of bubbling hot water which was later explained to me as being a way of releasing the muscles that were refusing to work after they had been placed in a position without movement for such a long time. I spent about an hour in the aerated hot water bath before being placed exhausted, back in a hospital bed. Most of the exhaustion was caused by all the pushing and shoving that the hospital doctors felt necessary to cure me!

However, I finally fell asleep only to be woken up at various intervals either by nurses giving me medicines or doctors pushing my joints around again. Whatever they were doing, it seemed to be working as after a few days, although still very stiff, my arms and legs were much easier for me to move around on my own and with truly little real pain.

The most uncomfortable and painful part of my body was my throat. It made it exceedingly difficult for me to speak and almost impossible to eat any solid foods. The nurses solved this problem by feeding me a small amount of ice-cream at regular intervals which seemed to have the effect of freezing my vocal cords whilst allowing me to say yes or no and making a few funny noises that, for the time being passed off as speech. However, it wasn't too long before my voice started to return, all be it with a squeaky abnormal sound.

Cardiff, United Kingdom

It was around 11:30 at night when a loud knocking on the front door of my Malefant Street home managed to wake my father up from a deep slumber. He, feeling as miserable as ever, possibly with some good reason in view of the hour staggering out of bed, went down the stairs and opened the front door of the property only to be greeted by five or six men who had gathered there.

"Good evening, does Brian Robson live here?"

"What?" asked my father, still half asleep.

"Brian Robson, does he live here?"

"He used to," answered my father, "he's in Australia right now!"

"He's not, he's in America," said one of the men.

"America? Well, thanks for letting us know," replied my father before closing the front door, turning around, and walking halfway back along the hallway. Suddenly stopping in his tracks, he turned back around toward the front door, stopped a second time, and then shaking his head to wake himself up completely, he opened the door a second time before asking them, "What did you just say?"

"Brian Robson's in America!"

The news reporters were now in the lounge of the house with yet another television crew knocking on the door and trying to get entry. They had been telling my father the story of me leaving Australia in a crate and were fishing for more information. He had already informed them that it was no good asking him questions as this was the first time that he had heard about it and, in all honesty, had less information than the reporters.

My mother came downstairs and was told the little information that was available at the time, she did what any Welsh woman of the day would have done; she made a pot of tea!

Chapter Thirty-Seven

"So, your name is Brian and you're from the UK; is that right?" asked one of the two immaculately dressed FBI officers who were standing at the side of my bed in the hospital ward.

I nodded a "yes" before telling him that I had been asked that by other officers the day before. He confirmed that he knew about my previous questioning, but it was common practice to go over it twice to make sure that they had the correct details. He then suggested that perhaps I could start by telling him what I was doing in a crate at Los Angeles Airport. Slowly, I started going over my story again with him just asking the occasional question. Two hours later, I had completed the narrative whilst he sat there with a big grin covering his face.

"That's quite some story," he said, "you're incredibly lucky to be with us and not in another kind of box!" I raised my eyebrows and nodded in reply before he asked, "Do you feel strong enough to speak with a television crew?"

Before I had a chance to answer his question, a group of people had entered the room carrying all sorts of equipment, and whilst most of the men were setting up their cameras, two of them started talking to me. After they introduced themselves telling me that they were reporters from two different television stations. One told me that his interview would be broadcast across the United States on evening news programmes whilst the other asked me if I had ever heard of 'The Telstar Satellite'. I said no I had never heard of it and he explained that it was a television and radio link that joined the States with Europe.

"Your home is in a place called Malefant Street, is that right?"

"Yes," I answered.

"Well, I believe that we have a crew there right now and what we are hoping to do is to have an interview with your parents for broadcast throughout the States whilst, at the same time, I want to interview you on the link to be broadcast throughout the UK on the BBC; think you can do it?"

Looking astonished, I asked him, "You mean we'll see Malefant Street here and they'll see us there?"

"You've got it, at least that's the idea!" he added.

"God, modern science, it's amazing, we'll have indoor toilets on aeroplanes next!" He laughed. "I think we have them now; you just need to be in a passenger cabin before you can use them!"

So the interviews went ahead, and I looked at the house where I was born for the first time in eleven months. It hadn't changed much, but it was nice to see it even if it was still a long way away.

Later, I had many visitors; some were newspaper or television reporters, and some were everyday Americans who came by to say hello and to wish me luck. Some even insisted that I accept a small amount of money to keep me going whilst I was in the States, and yet others were immigrants who had settled in the US after migrating from the UK; they thought that they were my mum or dad and kept telling me how brave I had been. I didn't quite see it that way but just felt that I had finally got my own back on Australia.

A few days later, I had fully recovered and was up and about on my own two wobbly feet. I was eating real food and generally feeling a lot better when I was told that the FBI had sent a car for me and that I would be going to their main Los Angeles office. Everyone was genuinely nice to me as I left the hospital to end up in the private office of the LA head of the Federal Bureau of Investigation.

To get into the room we had to pass through an outside office that was jam-packed with people who, I later found out, were once again, all reporters. However, we got through the mass, and as we entered the inner sanctum into the boss's office the press forged forward and entered with us.

A large, smiling, immaculately-dressed man quickly stood up from behind his desk and told everyone, except for me, to wait in the room outside before he shook my hand and told me to take a seat on the sofa. After the others had left, he sat down next to me. Still smiling, he explained that we had a few problems to sort out; the first of which was to get Pan American to agree on where they would be sending me next.

I asked him why Pan American would be sending me anywhere as I had sent the crate with Qantas? He told me that as the flight the crate had been originally booked on was full, the freight people in Sydney had used the next available flight which was the Pan American carrier. As they had flown me into the US, they were obligated by US law to fly me out again. They had two choices; one was to send me on to London and the other to fly me back to Australia. "However," he said, "it's up to them." I began to understand now how I ended up in America by travelling the Pacific route as opposed to the Asian route which, I had booked with Qantas.

He went back to his desk and after sitting down and making a phone call, he chatted to who was on the other end of the line and put the receiver back down, before speaking with me again, "Your luck is well in; they're going to fly you to London on this afternoon's flight!"

It was all I could do to hold back the tears, but these were tears of joy. I couldn't have even contemplated the thought of going back to Australia; not after all I had been through! Under my breath, I thanked God for Pan American Airlines.

"Are you happy now?" He asked with a smile.

"Yes, very," I replied with a big grin.

"I'm pleased for you; have you had a good time in the States?"

"I haven't seen much of it, but what I have seen was very good and everyone has been so helpful!"

"Good, now I want you to do something for me, will you?"

"Of course, what do you want me to do?"

He told me that my travels had caused a lot of publicity worldwide and it would help him and the FBI if we could play a little game with the press. He would invite them all into the office and then pretend to phone Pan American before telling me again that I was going to London. I would break into a big grin and thank him and his office for all the work they had put into the case.

"Would you do that?"

"Sure, I will," I answered.

"Good, and then later I'll personally take you to the airport to say goodbye. Oh, just one more thing, you don't have a passport, is that right?" I nodded my head in confirmation with doubts starting to creep into my head that this was now going to change the plans. The anxiety must have shown on my face because he told me not to worry and that he would fix that up.

Picking up the phone a second time, he spoke to the British Embassy who informed him that it would take up to two or three weeks to get a passport for me to travel. In his American way and with a grin, he told them not to bother as he would send me back that afternoon without one. If only I had known him in Australia!

So, that's what happened; the press took photographs and filmed whilst we acted the phone conversations out. It went down rather well, so I heard later!

The drive to the airport was more like a sightseeing trip with the FBI boss man and the car driver pointing out various places of interest. Following us was a press van full of news broadcasters filming everything that moved or anything that looked as though it was about too! It appeared to me that I had, over a short period of time, gone from being a nobody who just wanted to go home into something of a minor celebrity.

We arrived at the airport, and I was being ushered into a room when my boss man friend suddenly noticed that I wasn't wearing any shoes on my feet. He asked me where they were, and I told him that someone had taken them off me when I was pulled from the crate.

"It's too late now," he grumbled, "but you should have told me; we could have got you a new pair!"

How was I supposed to know that? Anyway, I didn't care much about shoes, I was going home! He however was insistent and somehow or other, he managed to get me a pair of slippers that were offered to airline passengers during a flight. They were bright blue and with a Pan American logo and, as he seemed quite pleased with himself, I kept thanking him and continued to wear them all the way to London.

"Are you ready to board now?" One of the Pan Am staff asked me. I nodded my head and then shook hands with all the officials and airline staff standing around and taking care of me.

"Don't forget to smile," my boss man friend reminded me as we walked between a large crowd of press and other people all wanting to shake my hand and say goodbye. Arriving at the door of the aircraft we turned around and the boss man and I shook hands. He slapped me on my back, wished me good luck and told me to have a safe flight. It was all over.

I was seated in a first-class window seat onboard an incredibly quiet aircraft and able to breathe a sigh of relief knowing that nothing could stop me going to the UK now.

Chapter Thirty-Eight

We were barely into the flight when the crew made an announcement welcoming everyone aboard and telling them that the first person ever to fly across the Pacific Ocean in a crate was flying with them and as was customary in that period, everyone clapped. During the flight, they became even more personal as many passengers came up to my seat and after congratulating me wanted to shake my hand. This was a bit too much as I had really thought that I had left that life behind and was just going home however, I obliged them and shook their hands.

I didn't want to be a minor celebrity, I just wanted to be myself and truthfully left completely alone. The longer the flight progressed the more people offered their hands to shake and the more embarrassed and shy I began to feel.

Sitting next to me in the aisle seat was a friendly older gentleman with much more experience than I had and quite apart from offering me advice for when we arrived in London, he offered me practical advice for use on the plane.

"If you want to be left alone and you see someone approaching, just close your eyes and pretend to be asleep!" It almost worked except that as they approached me, with me pretending my eyes were closed, I couldn't help giggling which sort of gave the game away.

Cardiff, United Kingdom

Whilst I was flying the Atlantic Ocean first-class the UK press was still hounding my family and neighbours back in Cardiff. Malefant Street had never seen such activity since the street party held to celebrate the Queen's Coronation in 1953. Television cameras and photographers were everywhere, and one struck lucky!

My father read the Daily Express every weekday for the horse racing page and was more than overly impressed when one of the reporters crowding my house introduced himself as working for that newspaper. He was further impressed when offered a car to take him to London to meet me in exchange for exclusive photographs of my arrival. He jumped at the offer—my mother couldn't go as she had to look after my younger brother—so he would go alone. At my father's suggestion the meeting would be arranged in a pub, and so they set off immediately so that he would be there for the pub's opening time oh, and later my arrival.

London, United Kingdom

We landed in London and the plane taxied to its parking spot at the airport. As they wheeled the steps up to the aircraft for the passengers to disembark, I could see through the window many newspaper reporters hanging around. I looked at my fellow passenger hoping for his help, and true to form, he was ready with an answer to my gaze.

"Don't worry, they only want your photograph but, don't let them take it, and then you'll control the situation and decide who to give it to."

"How do I stop them?"

He handed me a newspaper. "Cover your face with this and just walk past them!" Then, with a chuckle, he wished me good luck and I made my way to the exit of the plane. Holding the newspaper, he had given me in front of my face, I bravely stepped off and walked into the crowd. I was saved from all their shouts asking for photographs by a man in uniform who welcomed me home and very politely told me he was an immigration officer, and could I spare him five minutes of my time?

We both walked, followed by the press, to an office in the terminal building where the reporters were locked outside. I felt worried as I didn't have a passport and I was sure that they would put me on the next plane out of the country. I must have looked nervous as the immigration official told me not to worry and he would only keep me a few minutes. We sat down and he asked me four or five questions such as where was I was born, what colour were the busses in Cardiff and how to get from place 'A' to place 'B'. Satisfied with my answers, he told me I was free to go and that they had arranged a press conference at the airport for me to meet the press. I asked if I had to go and meet them and he answered, "No, but it would be better if you did as that will get them off your back."

Nodding my head, I let him lead me along the corridor to where the conference had been arranged. Along the way we were joined by another man who whispered to me that he was a Daily Express reporter and that he had my father in a pub and that I shouldn't say too much at the press meeting as the 'Express' were going to buy my story and he would take me to meet my father later. As soon as he mentioned the word 'pub' I knew that he didn't mean that they had taken my father as a prisoner, and so I agreed to go along with him.

I didn't say much at the press conference as I just wanted to get out of there.

The Daily Express reporter was very chatty on the drive down to the 'Red Lion Pub' in High Wickham and promised that for exclusive photographs the newspaper would pay me one hundred and fifty pounds, quite a lot of money in those days. After we arrived at the pub, we went into the bar only to be met by my father—proving that they weren't telling me lies—and a few more reporters with a photographer from the newspaper were also present. We posed with my father giving me a few hugs whilst they took their photographs before the photographer left to get his work developed for the morning edition of the paper.

I was offered a beer which I refused, then we all sat down, and they drank beer after beer and interviewed me at the same time as they were drinking.

After getting fed up and remembering my friend's advice, the one who had sat next to me on the plane, I pretended to fall asleep whilst they carried on drinking. This didn't seem to work as, ignoring me, they appeared to be heading for a party. I finally gave up on the sleeping idea and just as they were about to order more beer I spoke up. "Am I free to do anything I want now?" I gingerly asked.

"Of course, you are, what do you want to do?"

"I want to go home!"